ADVANCE PRAISE FOR
The Buddhist Chef's Homestyle Cooking

"Whether you're plant-based or simply plant-curious, *The Buddhist Chef's Homestyle Cooking* is a must-have on any shelf. Jean-Philippe crafts the perfect balance of wholesome everyday eats and comforting treats for special occasions. This cookbook is bursting with creativity and proves that a vegan diet is far from bland or boring!"

—**CAITLIN SHOEMAKER**, creator of From My Bowl and author of *Simply Delicious Vegan*

"J-P masterfully brings together the best of homestyle and professional cooking in this accessible collection of inspired recipes. His simple yet flavor-forward approach is ideal for those of us who want to eat deliciously with minimal fuss. This is a cookbook for the whole family."

—**ANNA PIPPUS**, author of *The Vegan Family Cookbook*

The Buddhist Chef's

Homestyle Cooking

SIMPLE, SATISFYING VEGAN
RECIPES FOR SHARING

BY JEAN-PHILIPPE CYR

appetite

by RANDOM HOUSE

Appetite by Random House® and colophon are registered trademarks of Penguin
Random House LLC.

Library and Archives of Canada Cataloguing in Publication is available upon request.
ISBN: 978-0-52-561236-0
eBook ISBN: 978-0-52-561237-7

Styling by Michael Linnington
Photography by Dominique Lafond
Cover and book design by Talia Abramson

Printed in China

Published in Canada by Appetite by Random House®, a division of Penguin Random
House Canada Limited

www.penguinrandomhouse.ca

10 9 8 7 6 5 4 3 2 1

appetite
by RANDOM HOUSE

Penguin
Random House
Canada

To my wife, who helps me through every part of the process.

Contents

INTRODUCTION

As far back as I can remember, food has been at the center of my family's life. My mom was an outstanding cook, and there was always a soup or pasta sauce boiling away, so we always had a reason to invite people over. Whether it was birthdays, holidays, or even just sunny days, our dinner table was always crowded. She was from a family of 16 siblings, so we never lacked guests hungry for her dishes that comforted the stomach as much as they comforted the soul. During our meals, conversations would spark around the table, with plenty of jokes and secrets being shared. It was as obvious to me then as it is now that food is the best way to bring people together. Around delicious food, tongues become untied, conversations go from small talk to knowing banter, and tablemates go from strangers to friends.

As a young teenager, I became comfortable enough in the kitchen to start preparing some of our family meals myself. I was so proud to serve dishes like boeuf bourguignon, which, if not perfect, was at the very least prepared with love. At 16, I became the de facto private chef for my group of friends. They favored my food over fast food, which was no simple feat, considering the way teenagers crave burgers and pizza. Cooking for my friends and family at such a young age taught me that creating memorable moments together was more important than the food itself. I also learned that for creating those special moments, no restaurant meal could ever rival a dinner shared with friends and family in the comfort of your own home. There's so much less pretension with home cooking—it's all about delicious, comforting food and quality conversation with family and friends! During my career in the restaurant industry, I continued to cook the same rustic food I liked to cook at home. I was offered positions in pretentious restaurants that served flashy food, but no thanks. I always favored authenticity and imperfection over precious, perfectly plated food lacking flavor.

When I was a professional chef, I traveled to Cambodia and Thailand. As many chefs do, I traveled to experience new flavors and techniques that I could incorporate into my cooking. To my surprise, while there certainly were many flavors I hadn't experienced before, there was a satisfying, rustic quality to much of what I ate that made me feel like I was right back at home. The way food was served also felt a lot like home: it was all about sharing. My time in Southeast Asia further reinforced that cooking is about bringing people together, not showing off. I also learned how to better balance flavors and how important acidity is to making other flavors shine. Since my travels, if a dish tastes like it's missing something, I turn to lemon juice or vinegar. It almost always does the trick!

In the not so distant past, it was all the rage in vegan cooking to make everything taste like soy sauce and soy sauce only. Unfortunately, soy sauce was often the only seasoning vegan cooks used, so there were a lot of bland, dry, uninteresting meals being served. One time, I was even served a single roasted sweet potato as a whole meal! Enough! After I adopted a vegan diet, I continued to cook dishes that were full of flavor and perfect for sharing with my friends and family. The bland, boring dishes of old-school hippy vegan cuisine would have no place in my kitchen.

In this book, I've drawn from all my experiences and lessons learned as a teenager, traveler, and professional chef to create recipes that show that vegan cooking can be just as appetizing and satisfying as any other style of cooking. Take my recipe for Vegan Fried Chicken (page 97), for example. You would never guess that it's made with mushrooms, and when people taste it, they won't believe it's not chicken! They'll have the same reaction to the Tofish & Chips (page 135), Tandoori Tofu (page 153), Cheesy Mushroom Gratin (page 55), Orange Tofu (page 164), and so many of the other recipes in this book. You don't even have to tell your family and friends the meal you're serving is vegan—it's just delicious food that they won't be able to stop eating. These are dishes that will truly please everyone, even those who have never tried vegan food, because they share the common denominator of all the world's best cuisines: flavor. If a dish is full of flavor, it doesn't matter whether it's vegan or not. It's just delicious.

THE BUDDHIST CHEF KITCHEN

PANTRY

Agar-agar is a gelling agent made from algae that is the perfect vegan replacement for animal-based gelatin. To activate agar-agar, you dissolve it in a liquid and bring it to a boil. As the mixture cools down it gels, just like Jell-O. There are two types of agar-agar on the market: powder and flakes. I used agar-agar powder for the recipes in this book; if you use agar-agar flakes, be sure to double the quantity to get similar results. It's very helpful for desserts like the Oreo Cheesecake (page 181).

Almonds in all their forms are a kitchen must-have. I sprinkle sliced almonds over muffins, transform slivered almonds into Almond Ricotta (page 149), and add almond flour to desserts, such as a Trio of Vegan Cupcakes (page 189–91). Almonds are so versatile!

Flours come in so many varieties, it can be hard to keep up. The flour I use most often is unbleached all-purpose flour, which is versatile and inexpensive. I also use two specialty flours. For recipes like my Vegan Fried Chicken (page 97), I use spelt flour, an ancient-grain flour that has a unique flavor and a low gluten content that makes the "chicken" extra crispy. For making seitan and other plant-based proteins, like my Tofish Burger with Tartar Sauce (page 131), I use vital wheat gluten flour. It has a very high gluten content, which helps to create the structure needed for plant-based proteins.

Himalayan black salt is a rock salt with a distinct sulfurous taste reminiscent of hard-boiled eggs, which is perfect for a Tofegg Sandwich (page 127). You can buy it online.

Liquid smoke is a condiment used in small quantities to add a smoky flavor in recipes like Tandoori Tofu (page 153) and Maple and Tempeh Baked Beans (page 17). You can usually find it in the condiment aisle, next to Worcestershire sauce.

Nutritional yeast is an inactive yeast used as a condiment in vegan cooking. As well as being rich in B-complex vitamins, it also adds a cheesy, savory flavor to recipes like Tofu with Creamy Mushroom Sauce and Kale Orzo (page 141) or even when sprinkled on top of popcorn. You can find it in stores in flake form. Don't confuse it with baking yeast or brewer's yeast!

Olive oil is healthier and more flavorful than vegetable oil. It can be used in salad dressings and for cooking, but it must be used carefully since it has a strong flavor and a low smoking point. Use extra-virgin for these recipes.

Quick-cooking oats are often associated with breakfast, but they can also be used as a binding agent in recipes for any time of day, such as Lentil Cretons (page 13) and veggie burgers. That said, what's better than a bowl of oatmeal to start the day?

Vegetable oil is a neutral-tasting oil I use for cooking and frying because of its high smoking point, meaning it can get quite hot without burning. Canola or sunflower oil can be used in place of vegetable oil.

PLANT-BASED DAIRY

Plant milks have become quite popular over the past few years, and several great options are now available in all grocery stores. I recommend using unsweetened soy milk in my recipes because of its neutral flavor, but most plant milks are interchangeable, including soy milk, oat milk, and almond milk. The only plant milk that should be used with caution is coconut milk, because it has a much higher fat content than other plant milks. Be careful, though: many plant milks are sweetened, which can significantly alter a recipe, so be sure to check the label at the grocery store to make sure you have the unsweetened variety. When I'm looking to add more richness to a dish, I also often use soy cream. Belsoy is my preferred brand.

Vegan butter is a non-dairy butter substitute made by combining water with a vegetable oil such as olive, avocado, coconut, or palm, or a combination of vegetable oils. It offers the same properties as regular butter, and I use it mostly in desserts. My favorite brand is Earth Balance.

Vegan cheeses are also experiencing a rapid increase in popularity and availability. I recently counted over 50 varieties at my local grocery store! Vegan cheese adds a comforting richness in some of my recipes, especially vegan mozzarella in baked dishes like Sweet Potato Enchiladas (page 81). Quality varies widely from brand to brand, so I recommend you try different ones to find your favorite. If you want a cheese for melting, look for an oil-based cheese, and if you're looking for a cheese to spread, look for a cashew-based cheese. As a general rule, it's best to invest in a higher-quality vegan cheese.

PLANT-BASED PROTEIN

Legumes are one of the most important sources of protein in a vegan diet. They're inexpensive and versatile, as well as good for you and the environment. Legumes are low in fat but high in protein and fiber, and they contain essential micronutrients. It's best to cook legumes from their dried form because the texture is better than canned, but you can't beat the convenience of canned legumes. Between you and me, you can't really taste a difference between the two.

These are some of the most commonly used legumes:

- Chickpeas
- Lentils (green, red, and black)
- Dried peas, split and whole
- Black beans
- Red kidney beans
- White beans

Mushrooms have a meaty texture and a unique flavor that are key to vegan cuisine. In this book, I use white button mushrooms, shiitake mushrooms, oyster mushrooms, and portobello mushrooms. Depending on the variety of mushroom, I like to fry them, cover them with melted vegan cheese, or toss them with different sauces. I encourage you to experiment with mushrooms—they'll become your best friend.

Plant-based meats like Beyond Meat and Impossible Burger are just as satisfying as animal proteins but have a gentler impact on the environment. Even though these products are easier on the environment, they are just as rich as animal protein, so I like to use them in rotation with lighter plant-based proteins.

Quinoa is a high-protein whole grain with a high iron content. It is excellent as a side dish or salad, among other uses. Quinoa is cooked just like rice, with a volume of water one and a half to two times the volume of quinoa. Note that quinoa grains are covered with a slightly bitter coating (called saponin) that must be removed by thorough rinsing with water before cooking.

Tempeh is a fermented soybean-based protein that has a more compact texture and a more pronounced flavor than tofu. It's not smooth, either—you can still see the soybeans and feel their crunch when you eat tempeh. Its taste is reminiscent of mushrooms, walnuts, and yeast and has lots of umami, the famous fifth fundamental taste. I love to use it in rich, savory preparations like my Walnut Bolognese Sauce (page 118) and Caramelized Onion Tempeh (page 121). You can find it in the frozen section of the grocery store.

Tofu is a high-protein, low-fat plant-based protein made from soybean milk. It is very versatile and has a neutral taste, which allows it to absorb the flavor of whatever you season it with. Tofu is available in different levels of firmness, from soft to extra-firm. For savory dishes, I suggest getting the firmest tofu you can find. The labeling can be confusing, so verify the tofu by touch. For example, firm or extra-firm tofu should have the same resistance when you press it as cheddar cheese.

EQUIPMENT

Blenders are very useful for pureeing foods, especially soups. Don't use a blender to replace a food processor, which is better for grinding or chopping ingredients. My favorite blender brand is Vitamix, which makes an expensive but extremely efficient blender.

Food processors are another essential tool for vegan cooks. They allow you to grind dry ingredients, as opposed to the blender, which requires liquid to thoroughly blend foods. Food processors have interchangeable blades that allow them to cut vegetables in many ways. Choose a food processor that corresponds to your needs: a student could likely make do with a smaller 7-cup (1.75 L) food processor, whereas a family of four will need one with a larger capacity.

Kitchen scales are helpful for ensuring consistency in cooking, particularly baking. Although both volume and weight allow for correct measurements, weighing solid ingredients will always be a more precise way to go.

Breakfasts

Lentil Cretons

Makes 2 cups (500 mL) | **Prep Time: 15 min** | **Cook Time: 25 min** | **Chill Time: 1 hour**

Breakfast is the most important meal of the day . . . along with lunch and dinner, in my humble opinion! Good news: these cretons can be enjoyed any time of day and are just as delicious on toast as they are in a sandwich. Cretons are a classic Quebecois pâté-like dish usually made from ground pork. It was one of my favorite dishes growing up, so of course I had to veganize it.

1 cup (200 g) dried green lentils, rinsed
3 tablespoons olive oil
1 large onion, minced
8 ounces (225 g) white button mushrooms, chopped
3 cups (750 mL) vegetable broth
3 tablespoons nutritional yeast
1 tablespoon maple syrup
1½ teaspoons salt
¼ teaspoon ground cloves
¼ teaspoon ground cinnamon
¼ teaspoon ground mustard
¼ teaspoon dried thyme
½ cup (45 g) quick-cooking oats

1. Grind the lentils in a coffee grinder or a blender. Set aside.

2. In a skillet over medium heat, heat the oil, then add the onion and mushrooms, and cook, stirring, for 7 minutes.

3. Stir in the lentils and the remaining ingredients, except the oats. Lower the heat, and simmer for 10 to 15 minutes, stirring frequently, until the lentils are cooked and the liquid is absorbed. Stir in the oats and cook for 4 minutes, stirring from time to time.

4. Transfer to a container and refrigerate for at least 1 hour before serving. Serve spread on toast or as part of a sandwich. The cretons will keep in an airtight container in the fridge for up to 5 days.

Veggie Pâté

Serves 12 | Prep Time: 25 min | Cook Time: 1 hour

Finding a tasty veggie pâté recipe is more difficult than it seems. Most produce a pasty, bland result that looks better suited for construction than dining. But my recipe is dependable, delicious, and easy to prepare, all thanks to the flavorful base of carrots, potatoes, and nutritional yeast. You'll never look for another veggie pâté recipe after tasting this one!

⅓ cup (80 mL) olive oil

1 onion, minced

3 stalks celery, minced

2 yellow-fleshed potatoes (about 10½ oz/300 g), peeled and grated

2½ cups (275 g) grated carrots

1 cup (160 g) unsalted sunflower seeds

⅔ cup (82 g) all-purpose flour

½ cup (30 g) nutritional yeast

1 tablespoon dried oregano

1 teaspoon dried basil

¾ teaspoon salt

Black pepper, to taste

3 tablespoons soy sauce

1 tablespoon apple cider vinegar

Bagels or bread, toasted, for serving

1. Preheat the oven to 375°F (190°C). Grease a 9 × 13-inch (23 × 33 cm) baking dish with oil or line with parchment paper.

2. In a skillet over medium-high heat, heat the oil, then add the onions and cook for 5 minutes, stirring from time to time. Add the celery, potatoes, and carrots, lower the heat to low, and cook for 8 minutes, stirring frequently.

3. Remove from the heat, add the remaining ingredients (except the bagels), and stir to combine.

4. In a food processor, blend half of the mixture until smooth, about 1 minute. Stir the blended mixture back into the remaining textured mixture to combine.

5. Transfer the mixture to the prepared baking dish and smooth out the top.

6. Bake for 45 minutes. Let cool before serving with bagels or toast. The pâté will keep in an airtight container in the fridge for up to 5 days.

Maple and Tempeh Baked Beans

Serves 8 | **Prep Time: 30 min** | **Soak Time: 12 hours** | **Cook Time: 3 to 4 hours**

Here's my mom's classic baked beans recipe. I adapted it by replacing pork with tempeh. This recipe takes a while to prepare, but you can freeze it, as my mother would say. There's nothing better than realizing you have a bounty of baked beans in your freezer when cold weather arrives!

2 cups (400 g) dried white beans
2 tablespoons vegetable oil
2 onions, minced
¼ cup (60 mL) maple syrup
3 tablespoons tomato paste
2 tablespoons miso paste
1 teaspoon mustard powder
1 teaspoon salt
Black pepper, to taste
Smoked Tempeh (below)
6 cups (1.5 L) vegetable broth, plus more as needed
Bread, toasted, for serving

1. Put the beans in a large bowl, then cover with cold water. Let soak for 12 hours, then rinse and drain. Set aside.

2. Preheat the oven to 325°F (160°C).

3. In an ovenproof pot or Dutch oven over medium heat, heat the oil, then add the onions and sweat for 5 minutes. Stir in the maple syrup, tomato paste, miso, mustard, salt, pepper, drained beans, and tempeh.

4. Add the broth and bring to a boil, then remove from the heat and cover with foil.

5. Bake for 3 to 4 hours, until the beans are tender, adding more broth if necessary. Serve with toast. The beans will keep in an airtight container in the fridge for up to 5 days.

SMOKED TEMPEH Cook Time: 10 min

3 tablespoons vegetable oil
1 package (8½ oz/240 g) tempeh, cut into small dice
1 cup (250 mL) vegetable broth
2 tablespoons maple syrup
2 tablespoons soy sauce
2 tablespoons ketchup
1 tablespoon liquid smoke

1. In a skillet over medium heat, heat the oil, then add the tempeh and sauté until golden brown, about 4 minutes.

2. Add the remaining ingredients and bring to a boil, then lower the heat and simmer until the liquid is fully absorbed, about 5 minutes.

Tex-Mex Brunch Plate

Serves 2 | Prep Time: 30 min | Cook Time: 25 min

When you're vegan, making breakfast is the biggest challenge. That, and making friends! To remedy the first issue, I suggest trying this lightly spicy Tex-Mex brunch plate, served with deliciously crunchy baby potatoes—and it might help you with the friends issue too.

Baby Potatoes:

1 jalapeño pepper, seeded and minced

1 tablespoon nutritional yeast

½ teaspoon garlic powder

½ teaspoon onion powder

½ teaspoon dried oregano

½ teaspoon salt

¼ teaspoon sweet paprika

Black pepper, to taste

3 tablespoons olive oil

1½ lbs (700 g) baby potatoes, halved

Tex-Mex Hash:

3 tablespoons olive oil

1 onion, minced

1½ cups (245 g) frozen corn kernels

1 can (14 oz/398 mL) black beans, rinsed and drained

2 cloves garlic, minced

1 jalapeño pepper, seeded and minced

1 teaspoon salt

½ teaspoon sweet paprika

¼ teaspoon ground cumin

Black pepper, to taste

1¼ cups (310 mL) vegetable broth

2 tablespoons tomato paste

1 teaspoon maple syrup

For the Baby Potatoes:

1. Preheat the oven to 400°F (200°C).

2. In a bowl, combine all the ingredients, except the potatoes. Add the potatoes and toss to coat. Transfer to a baking sheet and spread out in a single layer.

3. Bake for 25 minutes, or until the potatoes are golden brown.

For the Tex-Mex Hash:

4. Meanwhile, in a skillet over medium heat, heat the oil, then add the onion and sauté for 5 minutes. Add the corn and beans, and cook for 3 minutes.

5. Add the garlic and jalapeño, and cook for 2 minutes. Add the remaining hash ingredients and bring to a boil, then lower the heat and simmer, stirring frequently, until the liquid is fully absorbed, about 4 minutes.

Recipe continues

To Serve:

Tomato, sliced
Avocado, sliced
Leaf lettuce leaves
Bread, toasted

To Serve:

6. Divide the hash and potatoes between the plates. Serve with tomatoes, avocado, lettuce and toast.

Buckwheat Bread with Raspberry-Chia Jam

Makes 1 loaf | Prep Time: 20 min | Proof Time: 1½ hours | Cook Time: 40 min

Let me confess something: I'm no good at baking bread. But, thankfully, I don't need to be with this failproof recipe. Who needs 36 different bread recipes when you've got one that works! By the way, this is also my mom's favorite recipe, and she'd been making bread from scratch for 50 years.

1⅔ cups (410 mL) warm water
2 tablespoons maple syrup
3 cups (375 g) all-purpose flour
1 cup (140 g) buckwheat flour
1 packet (¼ oz/8 g) instant yeast
1 teaspoon salt
3 tablespoons quick-cooking oats
Raspberry-Chia Jam, for serving

1. In a small bowl, whisk together the water and maple syrup.

2. In a large bowl, whisk together the flours, yeast, and salt. Add the wet ingredients to the dry ingredients. Use a fork to start mixing the ingredients together, then mix with your hands for 1 minute, until a sticky ball forms.

3. Cover the bowl with a clean, damp kitchen towel. Let the dough rise for 1 hour in a warm, draft-free spot.

4. Transfer the dough to a lightly floured work surface, then knead for 1 minute. Sprinkle with more flour if needed.

5. Transfer the dough to a 5 × 9-inch (13 × 23 cm) loaf pan and let rise for 30 minutes.

6. Meanwhile, preheat the oven to 375°F (190°C).

7. Brush the dough with water and sprinkle with the oats.

8. Bake for 40 minutes. Remove from the pan, transfer to a wire rack, and let cool completely.

9. Slice and serve with the Raspberry-Chia Jam. The bread will keep in an airtight container for up to 5 days.

Recipe continues

RASPBERRY-CHIA JAM

Makes 1½ cups (375 mL) | Prep Time: 25 min | Cook Time: 25 min | Chill Time: 1 hour

4 cups (500 g) frozen raspberries
½ cup (125 mL) maple syrup
1 tablespoon lemon juice
2 tablespoons chia seeds

1. In a saucepan, bring the raspberries, maple syrup, and lemon juice to a boil. Lower the heat and simmer for 25 minutes, whisking frequently.

2. Remove from the heat and stir in the chia seeds. Let cool completely before transferring to airtight jars. Refrigerate for at least 1 hour before eating. The jam will keep in in the fridge for up to 7 days.

Healthy Oatmeal Cookies

Makes 12 cookies | Prep Time: 15 min | Cook Time: 20 min

If you follow me on social media, you're probably tired of seeing me eat these healthy cookies—I share them so much they've almost become my signature recipe. But I can't stop eating them for the energy boost they give. Could it be the cookies I eat that allow me to do 45 minutes of non-stop Zumba? Perhaps.

2 ripe bananas
¼ cup (60 mL) peanut butter
¼ teaspoon ground cinnamon
Pinch of salt
2 cups (180 g) quick-cooking oats
12 pitted dates

1. Preheat the oven to 375°F (190°C). Line a baking sheet with parchment paper.

2. In a bowl, mash the bananas with a fork. Add the peanut butter, cinnamon, and salt, and stir to combine. Stir in the oats.

3. Using two spoons, divide the cookie dough into 12 mounds and set 1 inch (2.5 cm) apart on the prepared baking sheet. Lightly press a date into each mound.

4. Bake for 20 minutes. Transfer the cookies to a wire rack and let cool. The cookies will keep in an airtight container at room temperature for up to 5 days.

Apple Muffins with Almond Crumble

Makes 12 muffins | Prep Time: 30 min | Cook Time: 25 min

When I was a kid, I would eat only the muffin tops, inarguably the best part of the muffin! I've somehow found a way to make muffin tops even better, with the addition of a crunchy almond streusel. That said, if I'd found a recipe as good as this back then, I would've learned to eat whole muffins, that's for sure!

Almond Crumble:

½ cup (57 g) slivered almonds
2 tablespoons packed brown sugar
2 tablespoons all-purpose flour
2 tablespoons quick-cooking oats
2 tablespoons vegetable oil
½ teaspoon lemon juice
Pinch of salt

Apple Muffins:

1¾ cups (220 g) all-purpose flour
½ cup (45 g) quick-cooking oats
1 teaspoon salt
1 teaspoon baking soda
1 teaspoon baking powder
½ teaspoon ground cinnamon
¼ teaspoon ground ginger
¾ cup (165 g) packed brown sugar
½ cup (125 mL) vegetable oil
½ cup (125 mL) unsweetened applesauce
½ cup (125 mL) unsweetened soy milk
1 tablespoon lemon juice
2 medium red apples, peeled and cut into very small dice

For the Almond Crumble:

1. In a bowl, combine all the crumble ingredients. Set aside.

For the Apple Muffins:

2. Preheat the oven to 350°F (180°C). Line a 12-cup muffin pan with paper cups or grease the cups generously with oil.

3. In a medium bowl, whisk together the flour, oats, salt, baking soda, baking powder, cinnamon, and ginger. Set aside.

4. In a large bowl, whisk together or use a hand mixer to beat together the brown sugar, oil, applesauce, soy milk, and lemon juice. Stir into the flour mixture until just combined. Add the diced apples and stir to combine.

5. Using a ⅓-cup (80 mL) ice-cream scoop, divide the batter among the prepared muffin cups. Sprinkle the crumble over the batter, then use the back of a spoon to lightly press down the crumble so it sticks to the batter.

6. Bake for 22 to 25 minutes, or until a toothpick inserted in the center of a muffin comes out clean. Remove from the pan, transfer to a wire rack, and let cool completely. Leftovers can be kept in an airtight container at room temperature or in the fridge for up to 5 days.

Salads

Broccoli and Cranberry Salad

Serves 4 | Prep Time: 15 min | Chill Time: 3 hours

I'm sure this recipe will quickly become a classic in your house. The sweetness from the cranberries wonderfully complements the flavor of the broccoli. The secret here is to prepare the salad a few hours, or even a full day, in advance. The resting period will soften the broccoli, making the texture of the salad a delight.

Dressing:

½ cup (125 mL) vegan mayonnaise
1 tablespoon apple cider vinegar
1 tablespoon maple syrup
1 teaspoon salt
½ teaspoon garlic powder
½ teaspoon onion powder

Salad:

1 large head broccoli, cut into florets
¼ red onion, minced
½ cup (55 g) dried cranberries
¼ cup (40 g) unsalted sunflower seeds

For the Dressing:

1. In a large bowl, whisk together all the dressing ingredients.

For the Salad:

2. Add the vegetables, cranberries, and sunflower seeds to the bowl with the dressing, then toss to combine.

3. Refrigerate for at least a few hours or up to 1 day before serving.

Macaroni Salad with Jalapeño-Marinated Tofu

Serves 6 | Prep Time: 30 min | Chill Time: 2 hours | Cook Time: 10 min

I love the way jalapeño peppers spice things up! On pizzas, I always add sliced jalapeños for a touch of heat. Try it, and let me know what you think! In this recipe, I use pickled jalapeños, which are a bit less spicy and also provide some acidity. And what can I say about the marinated tofu? I dare you not to eat half of it before making the salad.

Marinated Tofu:

8 oz (225 g) firm tofu, diced

7 or 8 pickled jalapeño pepper rounds (about 2 tablespoons), drained and minced

2 cloves garlic, peeled and smashed

1 cup (250 mL) water

¼ cup (60 mL) apple cider vinegar

1 tablespoon olive oil

1 tablespoon maple syrup

1 tablespoon jalapeño pickling liquid

2 teaspoons salt

2 teaspoons onion powder

1 teaspoon dried oregano

Pinch of ground chipotle pepper

Dressing:

½ cup (125 mL) vegan mayonnaise

½ cup (125 mL) soy cream

2 tablespoons lime juice

1 tablespoon maple syrup

2 teaspoons garlic powder

1 teaspoon onion powder

1 teaspoon dried oregano

¾ teaspoon salt

½ teaspoon black pepper

Salad:

10½ ounces (300 g) dried macaroni pasta

20 cherry tomatoes, halved

2 stalks celery, thinly sliced

1 cup (165 g) frozen corn kernels, thawed

¼ cup (15 g) fresh parsley, minced

For the Marinated Tofu:

1. Add all the tofu ingredients to a 1-quart (1 L) airtight jar. Close the jar and shake to combine.

2. Refrigerate for at least 2 hours to marinate. Remove the garlic cloves before using. The marinated tofu will keep in the fridge for up to 5 days.

For the Dressing:

3. In a bowl, whisk together all the dressing ingredients to a smooth consistency. Set aside.

For the Salad:

4. Cook the pasta according to the package directions. Rinse under cold water, drain, and refrigerate until needed.

5. In a large bowl, combine all the salad ingredients. Add the marinated tofu with its liquid and the dressing, and toss to combine.

Trio of Dressings

Prep Time: 30 min

If there's one condiment you should prepare from scratch, it's salad dressing. I have a hard time understanding why so many people still buy industrially made dressings in supermarkets! It's so easy to make your own, and it's often less expensive and better tasting. These dressings are perfect for all kinds of salads, from a simple green salad to a hearty bean salad or a classic potato salad. They will keep in an airtight container in the fridge for up to 5 days.

RANCH-STYLE DRESSING Makes 1¼ cups (310 mL)

½ cup (125 mL) vegan mayonnaise
½ cup (125 mL) soy cream
¼ cup (15 g) minced chives

2 teaspoons onion powder
1 teaspoon garlic powder
¾ teaspoon black pepper

½ teaspoon salt
4 teaspoons apple cider vinegar
2 teaspoons maple syrup

MUSTARD, BALSAMIC, AND MAPLE DRESSING Makes ½ cup (125 mL)

¼ cup (60 mL) vegan mayonnaise
2 tablespoons maple syrup

2 tablespoons balsamic vinegar
1 tablespoon Dijon mustard

1 teaspoon salt
Black pepper, to taste

RELISH-MUSTARD DRESSING Makes ¾ cup (180 mL)

¼ cup (60 mL) vegan mayonnaise
2 green onions, minced
½ teaspoon salt
Black pepper, to taste

2 tablespoons soy cream
1 tablespoon apple cider vinegar
1 tablespoon maple syrup
1 tablespoon whole-grain mustard

1 tablespoon sweet relish
½ teaspoon hot sauce, such as
  Frank's RedHot

1. In a large bowl, whisk together all the dressing ingredients.

Quinoa Salad

Serves 2 | Prep Time: 15 min | Cook Time: 20 min | Rest Time: 20 min

Did you know that quinoa is the fruit of a plant in the same family as spinach and beets? And that quinoa has twice the fiber of pasta, and three times that of rice? And that quinoa is, in fact, delicious? These are just some of the excellent reasons why you should make this simple, nutritious, high-protein salad.

Quinoa:

2 cups (500 mL) water
1 cup (170 g) quinoa, rinsed

Dressing:

Juice from ½ lemon
2 tablespoons balsamic vinegar
1 tablespoon olive oil
1 tablespoon harissa paste
1 tablespoon maple syrup
Salt and black pepper, to taste

Salad:

1 can (14 oz/398 mL) chickpeas, rinsed and drained
1 tomato, diced
1 bunch (25 g) fresh parsley, chopped
¼ cup (33 g) raisins

For the Quinoa:

1. Pour the water into a saucepan, stir in the quinoa, then cover and set over medium-high heat. Bring to a boil, then lower the heat and simmer for 20 minutes, or until the water is fully absorbed.

2. Remove from the heat and let rest, covered, for 20 minutes, then use a fork to fluff up the quinoa.

For the Dressing:

3. Meanwhile, in a small bowl, whisk together all the dressing ingredients.

For the Salad:

4. In a large bowl, toss the quinoa with the salad ingredients and dressing.

Appetizers, Bites, and Sides

Zucchini Fritters with Tzatziki

Makes 10 fritters | Prep Time: 30 min | Rest Time: 15 min | Cook Time: 20 min

Would you be surprised to learn that zucchini is a fruit? I was too. Make sure not to add it to fruit salad, though! Fruit or not, I find it's best to turn zucchini into delicious fritters and serve them with a bright, fresh tzatziki.

Tzatziki:

½ cup (125 mL) vegan mayonnaise
2 tablespoons soy cream
⅓ English cucumber, finely diced
2 teaspoons minced fresh dill
¾ teaspoon onion powder
½ teaspoon maple syrup
¼ teaspoon salt
Black pepper, to taste

Fritters:

6 sun-dried tomatoes, minced
3 zucchini, grated
3 green onions, minced
2 cloves garlic, minced
20 fresh basil leaves, minced
2 teaspoons minced fresh dill
3 tablespoons nutritional yeast
1 teaspoon dried oregano
1 teaspoon baking powder
¾ teaspoon salt
½ teaspoon ground cumin
½ teaspoon red pepper flakes
Black pepper, to taste
2 teaspoons maple syrup
1 cup (125 g) all-purpose flour
¼ cup (60 mL) olive oil (approx.)
Lemon wedges, for serving

For the Tzatziki:

1. In a bowl, whisk together all the tzatziki ingredients. Cover and chill in the fridge until ready to serve.

For the Fritters:

2. In a large bowl, combine the sun-dried tomatoes, zucchini, green onions, garlic, basil, and dill. Add the yeast, oregano, baking powder, salt, cumin, red pepper flakes, black pepper, and maple syrup, and stir until thoroughly combined.

3. Preheat the oven to 350°F (180°C). Grease a baking sheet with oil.

4. Add the flour to the fitter mixture and stir to combine. Let the batter rest for 15 minutes. Stir the batter again before cooking.

5. In a skillet over medium heat, heat the oil, then drop ⅓ cup (75 g) of the batter per fritter into the hot oil, cooking 3 to 4 fritters at a time until golden brown, about 2 minutes on each side. Add oil between batches as necessary. As they are completed, transfer the browned fritters to the prepared baking sheet.

6. Bake the fritters for 8 minutes, until cooked through.

7. Serve with the tzatziki, with lemon wedges on the side for squeezing over the top.

Roasted Cauliflower with Truffle Oil Mayonnaise

Serves 4 | Prep Time: 20 min | Cook Time: 30 min

When I create a new recipe, I always ask myself if I would serve it to friends and family. In this case, the answer is a resounding *yes*! I've worked in high-end restaurants in the past, and I realized that the main differences between a homestyle dish and a posh dish are the presentation and the number of garnishes on the plate. But those fancy trimmings don't really matter—it's the combination of flavors that produces that wow factor! In this recipe, the roasted cauliflower is delicious on its own, but if you combine it with the truffle oil mayonnaise, pine nuts, and pomegranate seeds, it becomes a dish worthy of the finest restaurants.

Roasted Cauliflower:

⅓ cup (80 mL) olive oil
4 teaspoons nutritional yeast
¾ teaspoon salt
Black pepper, to taste
1 large head cauliflower, cut into florets

Truffle Oil Mayonnaise:

1 teaspoon garlic powder
½ teaspoon dried oregano
½ teaspoon truffle oil
¼ teaspoon ground chipotle pepper
¼ teaspoon salt
Black pepper, to taste
¼ cup (60 mL) vegan mayonnaise
¼ cup (60 mL) soy cream
2 teaspoons lime juice
2 teaspoons maple syrup

To Serve:

⅓ cup (50 g) pine nuts
2 tablespoons minced chives
Seeds from ½ pomegranate

For the Roasted Cauliflower:

1. Preheat the oven to 400°F (200°C).

2. In a large bowl, combine the oil, yeast, salt, and pepper. Add the cauliflower florets and toss to coat. Transfer to a baking sheet and spread out in a single layer.

3. Bake for 30 minutes, or until the florets are golden brown.

For the Truffle Oil Mayonnaise:

4. Meanwhile, in a bowl, whisk together all the mayonnaise ingredients. Set aside.

To Serve:

5. In a skillet over medium-high heat, toast the pine nuts for 2 minutes, stirring continuously, until golden brown.

6. Transfer the roasted cauliflower to a serving dish. Drizzle with the truffle oil mayonnaise and garnish with the toasted pine nuts, chives and pomegranate seeds.

Maple Roasted Brussels Sprouts

Serves 4 | Prep Time: 20 min | Cook Time: 20 min

When I was a kid, I much preferred chocolate to Brussels sprouts. Despite what you might think, that's still the case today. However, when I do crave Brussels sprouts, I like to roast them until golden brown and caramelized, then toss them in a surprising maple and balsamic vinegar sauce to create this tasty and elegant dish.

Brussels Sprouts:

6 cups (650 g) Brussels sprouts
¼ cup (60 mL) olive oil
2 tablespoons nutritional yeast
½ teaspoon garlic powder
¼ teaspoon salt
Black pepper, to taste

Maple Balsamic Sauce:

3 tablespoons maple syrup
2 tablespoons balsamic vinegar
2 teaspoons soy sauce
½ teaspoon hot sauce, such as Frank's RedHot
Black pepper, to taste
½ teaspoon cornstarch mixed with 2 teaspoons water

To Serve:

⅓ cup (80 mL) slivered almonds or toasted pine nuts
Minced chives

For the Brussels Sprouts:

1. Preheat the oven to 425°F (220°C).

2. Cut off the stem of the Brussels sprouts, then slice them in half vertically.

3. In a large bowl, combine the oil, yeast, garlic powder, salt, and pepper. Add the Brussels sprouts and toss to coat. Transfer to a baking sheet and spread out in a single layer.

4. Bake for 18 minutes, tossing halfway through, or until the sprouts are golden brown.

For the Maple Balsamic Sauce:

5. Meanwhile, in a small saucepan, combine all the sauce ingredients, except the cornstarch mixture. Bring to a boil over high heat, then whisk in the cornstarch mixture. Lower the heat to medium and cook for 1 minute, stirring constantly, or until the sauce thickens.

To Serve:

6. Transfer the roasted Brussels sprouts to a large bowl, add the maple balsamic sauce, and toss to combine. Garnish with the almonds and chives.

Buffalo Cauliflower

Serves 4 | **Prep Time: 30 min** | **Cook Time: 50 min**

When I became a vegan, I discovered the magic of roasting cauliflower. Roasting brings out the vegetable's lovely sweetness, something that boiling does not. The secret for this recipe is to spread the cauliflower florets all over a baking sheet covered with parchment paper (or a silicon mat). Don't ever oil or grease the sheet instead! This recipe makes every day Super Bowl Sunday!

1 cup (250 mL) unsweetened soy milk

1 cup (125 g) all-purpose flour

1 tablespoon paprika

2 teaspoons garlic powder

2 teaspoons onion powder

1 teaspoon salt

¼ teaspoon black pepper

1 large head cauliflower, cut into florets

2 tablespoons vegan butter

½ cup (125 mL) hot sauce, such as Frank's RedHot

Aïoli (page 124), for serving

1. Preheat the oven to 450°F (230°C). Line a baking sheet with parchment paper.

2. In a bowl, whisk together the soy milk, flour, paprika, garlic powder, onion powder, salt, and pepper. Dip each cauliflower floret into the batter to fully coat. Transfer to the prepared baking sheet and spread out in a single layer.

3. Bake for 25 minutes, or until the florets are golden brown and crunchy.

4. In a small saucepan over low heat, melt the vegan butter, then stir in the hot sauce.

5. Transfer the baked cauliflower florets to a large bowl. Add the hot sauce mixture and toss to coat.

6. Return the florets to the baking sheet, spreading them in a single layer. Bake for 25 minutes.

7. Serve with the aïoli.

Cognac Mushroom Mousse

Serves 6 | Prep Time: 20 min | Cook Time: 15 min

In another life, I prepared terrines, foie gras, and pâtés. I've changed a lot since then, but my love for terrines has remained—so much so that I've created this elegant mushroom mousse, which has nothing to envy of its fine-dining counterparts. As a bonus, it couldn't be easier to prepare!

Mushroom Mousse:

2 tablespoons olive oil

8 ounces (225 g) white button mushrooms, minced

1 shallot, minced

2 tablespoons cognac or brandy

¼ cup (60 mL) soy cream

1 tablespoon nutritional yeast

½ teaspoon salt

¼ teaspoon dried rosemary

¼ teaspoon mustard powder

Black pepper, to taste

1 tablespoon maple syrup

1 teaspoon lemon juice

To Serve:

2 tablespoons olive oil

6 slices baguette (each about ½ inch/1 cm thick)

For the Mushroom Mousse:

1. In a skillet over medium-high heat, heat the oil, then add the mushrooms and shallots, and cook, stirring, for about 8 minutes, or until the mushrooms are tender. Deglaze with the cognac and bring to a boil while stirring.

2. Add the remaining mousse ingredients and cook for 2 minutes over low heat, stirring continuously.

3. Transfer the mousse to a bowl and use an immersion blender to blend it to a smooth consistency. The mousse will keep in an airtight container in the fridge for up to 4 days.

To Serve:

4. In a skillet over medium-high heat, heat the oil, then add the baguette slices and toast on both sides until golden brown. Serve with the mushroom mousse.

Naan

Makes 4 breads | **Prep Time: 15 min** | **Proof Time: 45 min** | **Cook Time: 15 min**

How can something so simple be so delicious? I'll never know: I'm too busy eating this delicious naan to figure it out. This recipe includes instructions for cooking the naan in a skillet (great!) or on the barbecue (even better!). What can I say, I'm a generous person. This is a perfect recipe for both summer happy hours and afternoon snacks, not to mention serving alongside your favorite curry!

Seasoning:

¼ cup (60 mL) olive oil
1½ teaspoons dried oregano

Naan:

2 cups (250 g) all-purpose flour (approx.)
1 packet (¼ oz/8 g) instant yeast
1 teaspoon salt
1 teaspoon baking powder
½ teaspoon baking soda
¾ cup (180 mL) warm water
⅓ cup (80 mL) olive oil, divided
3 tablespoons soy cream
1 teaspoon maple syrup
½ teaspoon apple cider vinegar

For the Seasoning:

1. In a small bowl, whisk together the oil and oregano. Set aside.

For the Naan:

2. In a large bowl, whisk together the flour, yeast, salt, baking powder, and baking soda.

3. In another bowl, whisk together the water, 2 tablespoons of the oil, soy cream, maple syrup, and vinegar.

4. Make a well in the center of the dry ingredients and pour in the wet ingredients. Use a fork to start mixing the ingredients together, then mix with your hands for about 1 minute, until a sticky ball forms, adding more flour if needed.

5. Cover the bowl with a clean, damp kitchen towel. Let the dough rise at room temperature for 45 minutes.

6. Lightly flour a work surface. Deflate the dough by punching it down with your fist, transfer to the floured work surface, then knead for 1 minute, adding more flour if needed.

7. Divide the dough into 4 equal parts. Use a rolling pin to roll each piece of dough into a oval, about 8 inches (20 cm) long.

8. In a skillet over medium-high heat, heat the remaining oil. Add the naan, 1 or 2 at a time, depending on the size of the pan. Cook each naan until golden brown, about 2 minutes on each side. You can also cook the naan on a grill over medium-high heat for 1½ minutes on each side.

9. While the breads are still warm, brush them with the seasoning mixture.

Maple-Glazed Mushroom Scallops

Serves 4 | Prep Time: 25 min | Cook Time: 30 min

King oyster mushrooms are my favorite mushrooms. They have a firm, meaty texture and a subtle nutty flavor that is unlike anything else. I especially like to turn them into "scallops." Give this recipe a try—you'll discover that the similarity in texture is striking.

Mushroom Scallops:

¼ cup (60 mL) olive oil
8 king oyster mushrooms, sliced into ¾ inch (2 cm) rounds
1 shallot, minced
¼ cup (40 g) pine nuts
2 cloves garlic, minced
¼ cup (60 mL) white wine
¾ cup (180 mL) vegetable broth
2 tablespoons maple syrup
1 tablespoon lemon juice
1 tablespoon miso paste
1 teaspoon balsamic vinegar
1 sheet nori, minced
¼ teaspoon mustard powder
¼ teaspoon salt
Pinch celery salt
Black pepper, to taste

Green Pea Puree:

1 cup (250 mL) vegetable broth
2 cups (260 g) frozen green peas
1 teaspoon lemon juice
¼ teaspoon salt
Black pepper, to taste

For the Mushroom Scallops:

1. In a skillet over medium-high heat, heat the oil, then add the mushrooms and shallots, and cook, stirring, until the mushrooms are lightly browned, about 10 minutes.

2. Add the pine nuts and garlic, and cook for 2 minutes, stirring frequently. Deglaze with the wine and bring to a boil while stirring.

3. Stir in the remaining scallop ingredients and bring back to a boil. Lower the heat and simmer for 5 minutes. Keep warm.

For the Green Pea Puree:

4. In a saucepan, combine the broth and the green peas. Bring to a boil, then lower the heat, cover, and simmer, stirring from time to time, until most of the liquid is absorbed, about 8 to 10 minutes. Stir in the lemon juice, salt, and pepper.

5. Use an immersion blender to blend until smooth, or transfer to a food processor and blend until smooth.

To Serve:

6. Divide the pea puree among four serving plates. Arrange the maple-glazed mushroom scallops over the puree.

Cheesy Mushroom Gratin

Serves 4 | Prep Time: 20 min | Cook Time: 25 min

Every month, new vegan cheeses appear on grocery store shelves, and they keep getting better and better. Make the most of them by preparing this irresistible mushroom gratin! There are few pairings better than the holy trinity of mushrooms, cream, and cheese.

3 tablespoons olive oil

1 onion, minced

2 portobello mushrooms, diced

8 ounces (225 g) white button mushrooms, finely chopped

4½ ounces (125 g) shiitake mushrooms, minced

2 cloves garlic, minced

2 tablespoons cognac or brandy (optional)

1¼ cups (310 mL) vegetable broth

1 tablespoon minced fresh sage

¾ teaspoon salt

½ teaspoon dried rosemary

½ teaspoon garlic powder

½ teaspoon dried basil

½ teaspoon mustard powder

Black pepper, to taste

2 teaspoons maple syrup

½ cup (125 mL) soy cream

2½ cups (225 g) grated vegan cheese

Bread, toasted, for serving

1. Preheat the oven to 450°F (230°C).

2. In a skillet over medium-high heat, heat the oil, then add the onions and all three types of mushrooms, and cook, stirring, for 6 minutes. Add the garlic and cook for 2 minutes, stirring frequently. Deglaze with the cognac (if using) and bring to a boil while stirring, then lower the heat and simmer for 1 minute.

3. Stir in the broth, sage, salt, rosemary, garlic powder, basil, mustard, pepper, and maple syrup. Bring to a boil, then lower the heat and simmer, stirring frequently, until the liquid is fully absorbed, about 5 minutes. Stir in the soy cream and cook for 1 minute.

4. Divide the mushroom mixture among 4 ramekins set on a baking sheet. Sprinkle vegan cheese over each ramekin, dividing evenly.

5. Bake for 10 minutes, or until the cheese is melted and golden brown. Serve with toast.

Bruschetta Portobellos

Serves 4 | Prep Time: 20 min | Cook Time: 15 min

I love portobello mushrooms for their meaty texture that you won't find in any other vegetable. All you need to do to bring out their lovely earthy flavor is to roast them in the oven or grill them on the barbecue. If you're not as big a portobello fan as I am, you can also serve the bruschetta in this recipe over toasted baguette slices. This super-fresh recipe is perfect for summer nights on the patio.

Roasted Portobellos:

4 large portobello mushrooms, stems removed
3 tablespoons olive oil
Pinch of salt
Pinch of black pepper
Pinch of garlic powder

Bruschetta:

1 shallot, minced
2 teaspoons nutritional yeast
½ teaspoon garlic powder
¼ teaspoon salt
2 tablespoons olive oil
2 tablespoons balsamic vinegar
2 teaspoons maple syrup
¼ teaspoon hot sauce, such as Tabasco
15 cherry tomatoes, diced
5 fresh basil leaves, minced

For the Roasted Portobellos:

1. Preheat the oven to 400°F (200°C). Grease a baking sheet with oil.

2. Set the mushrooms on the prepared baking sheet, then brush them with the oil. Sprinkle evenly with salt, pepper, and garlic powder.

3. Bake for 15 minutes.

For the Bruschetta:

4. Meanwhile, combine all the bruschetta ingredients, except the tomatoes and basil. Add the tomatoes and stir to combine.

5. Place a roasted mushroom on each of four serving plates. Top each portobello with one-quarter each of the bruschetta and basil.

Soups

Creamy Spinach Soup

Serves 6 | Prep Time: 15 min | Cook Time: 45 min

I don't like my soups to be bland and watery. I like them hearty and nourishing! The most important task when making this soup is to find someone to peel the potatoes for you—unfortunately, this is usually my job at home. Once the potatoes are peeled, all you need to do is to combine the ingredients, bring them to a boil, and you're just about done! Heavy cream is usually added to this kind of soup, but in this recipe, cashews provide an incredible richness and creaminess.

Creamy Spinach Soup:

3 tablespoons olive oil

2 onions, minced

3 yellow-fleshed potatoes (about 1 lb/450 g), peeled and diced

16 cups (280 g) baby spinach

7 cups (1.8 L) vegetable broth

1¼ cups (175 g) cashews

¼ cup (15 g) nutritional yeast

1 teaspoon garlic powder

1 teaspoon dried oregano

1 teaspoon salt

Black pepper, to taste

Croutons:

3 tablespoons olive oil

½ baguette, cut into cubes

1½ tablespoons nutritional yeast

½ teaspoon garlic powder

½ teaspoon dried oregano

Pinch of salt

To Serve:

Handful of chives, minced

For the Creamy Spinach Soup:

1. In a large pot over medium heat, heat the oil, then add the onions and cook, stirring, for 5 minutes. Stir in the remaining soup ingredients and bring to a boil, then lower the heat and simmer for 40 minutes.

For the Croutons:

2. Meanwhile, in a skillet over medium-high heat, heat the oil, then add the bread cubes and cook, stirring frequently, for 5 minutes, or until they start to brown. Add the remaining ingredients and cook, stirring, for 1 to 2 minutes, or until the croutons are golden brown. Remove from the heat and set aside.

To Serve:

3. Using a slotted spoon, transfer about 1½ cups (375 mL) of the vegetables from the soup to a bowl.

4. Using an immersion blender in the pot, or transferring the soup to a blender, blend the soup until smooth. Stir in the reserved vegetables.

5. Divide the soup among six bowls and garnish with the croutons and chives. Leftover soup can be stored in the fridge in an airtight container for up to 4 days. Reheat in a saucepan over medium heat for about 5 minutes, or until hot.

Creamy Tomato Soup

Serves 6 | Prep Time: 35 min | Cook Time: 45 min

Ask people what their favorite comfort food is and they'll often mention tomato soup. Simple and hearty, this soup is the perfect companion to a grilled cheese sandwich—made with vegan cheese, of course. It's garnished with croutons and basil for an elegant presentation. Roasted red bell peppers add an irresistible, slightly smoky edge to the soup, making it even more memorable.

Cashew Cream:

1 cup (140 g) cashews
2 cups (500 mL) vegetable broth
⅓ cup (20 g) nutritional yeast
1 teaspoon dried basil
1 teaspoon dried oregano
1 teaspoon garlic powder
1 teaspoon salt
Black pepper, to taste
1 tablespoon maple syrup
1 teaspoon apple cider vinegar

Tomato Soup:

3 tablespoons olive oil
1 onion, minced
2 yellow-fleshed potatoes (about 10½ oz/300 g), peeled and diced
1 can (28 oz/796 mL) diced tomatoes, with juice
1 jar (12 oz/340 mL) roasted red bell peppers, drained, rinsed, and finely chopped
4 cups (1 L) vegetable broth

To Serve:

Fresh basil leaves, minced
Croutons (page 60)

For the Cashew Cream:

1. Soak the cashews in boiling water for 15 minutes. Drain.

2. Add the soaked cashews and the remaining cashew cream ingredients to a blender and blend until smooth. Set aside.

For the Tomato Soup:

3. In a large pot over medium heat, heat the oil, then add the onions and cook, stirring, for 5 minutes. Stir in the cashew cream and the remaining soup ingredients. Bring to a boil, then lower the heat and simmer for 40 minutes.

4. Using a slotted spoon, transfer about 1½ cups (375 mL) of the vegetables from the soup to a bowl.

5. Using an immersion blender in the pot, or transferring the soup to a blender, blend the soup until smooth. Stir in the reserved vegetables.

To Serve:

6. Divide the soup among six bowls and garnish with the basil and croutons. Leftover soup can be stored in the fridge in an airtight container for up to 4 days. Reheat in a saucepan over medium heat for about 5 minutes, or until hot.

Tex-Mex Soup

Serves 6 | Prep Time: 20 min | Cook Time: 55 min

This soup has personality in spades! Sweet potatoes, corn, coconut milk, cumin—see what I mean? It's flavor town! Serve me this soup with a thick slice of fresh bread, and I'll be the happiest man in the world. Don't forget to garnish the soup with perfectly ripe diced avocado: it makes it even better.

3 tablespoons olive oil

1 onion, minced

2 yellow-fleshed potatoes (about 10½ oz/300 g), peeled and diced

1 sweet potato (about 14 oz/400 g), peeled and diced

1 jalapeño pepper, seeded and minced

1 cup (165 g) frozen corn kernels

5 cups (1.25 L) vegetable broth

1 can (14 oz/398 mL) diced tomatoes, with juice

1 can (14 oz/398 mL) coconut milk

1 teaspoon ground cumin

1 teaspoon sweet paprika

1 teaspoon salt

¾ teaspoon ground chipotle pepper

Black pepper, to taste

To Serve:

Fresh cilantro leaves

Avocado, diced

Lime, sliced

1. In a large pot over medium heat, heat the oil, then add the onions and cook, stirring, for 5 minutes. Stir in the remaining ingredients and bring to a boil, then lower the heat and simmer for 50 minutes.

2. Using an immersion blender in the pot, or transferring the soup to a blender, blend the soup until smooth.

To Serve:

3. Divide the soup among six bowls and garnish with cilantro, avocado, and lime. Leftover soup can be stored in the fridge in an airtight container for up to 4 days. Reheat in a saucepan over medium heat for about 5 minutes, or until hot.

Vegan Tuscan Soup

Serves 6 | Prep Time: 35 min | Cook Time: 40 min

Creamy, luxurious soups don't always need to be pureed. This recipe still packs the same decadent punch, while also including nice hearty chunks of vegetables. The creamy texture from the cashew cream and the aroma from the fresh herbs make this soup an incredibly comforting dish.

Cashew Cream:

1 cup (140 g) cashews
2 tablespoons nutritional yeast

Tuscan Soup:

2 tablespoons olive oil
4 vegan sausages
4 cloves garlic, minced
1 onion, minced
1 tablespoon dried basil
1 tablespoon dried oregano
1 teaspoon salt
½ teaspoon dried thyme
3 yellow-fleshed potatoes (about 15 oz/425 g), diced
6 cups (1.5 L) vegetable broth
4 cups (50 g) chopped kale
Croutons (page 60), to garnish

For the Cashew Cream:

1. Soak the cashews in boiling water for 15 minutes. Drain.

2. Add the soaked cashews, 1 cup (250 mL) water, and the yeast to a blender and blend until smooth. Set aside.

For the Tuscan Soup:

3. In a large pot over medium heat, heat the oil, then add the sausages and break them up using a spatula. Increase the heat to medium-high and cook, stirring, for 3 minutes.

4. Add the garlic and onions, lower the heat to medium, and cook, stirring frequently, for 4 minutes. Stir in the basil, oregano, and salt, then the potatoes and broth. Bring to a boil, then lower the heat and simmer for 20 minutes.

5. Stir in the cashew cream and kale, and cook for 10 minutes.

6. Divide the soup among six bowls and garnish with croutons. Leftover soup can be stored in the fridge in an airtight container for up to 4 days. Reheat in a saucepan over medium heat for about 5 minutes, or until hot.

Butternut Squash Soup

Serves 6 | Prep Time: 20 min | Cook Time: 45 min

This is my favorite fall soup! It's so easy to prepare and incredibly delicious. Butternut squash is an underrated vegetable, in my humble opinion. People are reluctant to buy it because it seems complicated to prepare. Let me tell you—it couldn't be easier. All you need to do is peel it using a vegetable peeler, slice it in half, seed it, and it's ready to be turned into any number of incredible creations. The sweet, nutty flavor of butternut squash works wonders in this creamy soup.

3 tablespoons olive oil

1 large onion, minced

3 yellow-fleshed potatoes (about 15 oz/425 g), peeled and diced

1 small butternut squash, peeled, seeded, and cut into small dice

1 cup (140 g) cashews

6 cups (1.5 L) vegetable broth

1 teaspoon salt

Black pepper, to taste

1. In a large pot over medium heat, heat the oil, then add the onions and cook, stirring, for 5 minutes. Stir in the remaining ingredients and bring to a boil, then lower the heat and simmer for 30 to 40 minutes, or until the vegetables are soft.

2. Using an immersion blender in the pot, or transferring the soup to a blender, blend the soup until smooth. Season to taste. Leftover soup can be stored in the fridge in an airtight container for up to 4 days. Reheat in a saucepan over medium heat for about 5 minutes, or until hot.

Carrot and Ginger Soup

Serves 6 | Prep Time: 40 min | Cook Time: 50 min

Carrots are such a common vegetable that we tend to forget how versatile and delightfully sweet they can be. If that weren't enough, they're also filled with beta-carotene, a powerful antioxidant. In this recipe, I turn carrots into an incredibly aromatic soup. Chopped ginger adds some heat, sambal oelek some spice, and coconut milk a lovely creaminess. Garnished with a chive and lime cream, this memorable dish promises to become a classic at your house too.

Chive and Lime Cream:

½ cup (125 mL) soy cream
¼ cup (60 mL) minced chives
2 tablespoons lime juice
1 teaspoon maple syrup
½ teaspoon salt
½ teaspoon garlic powder
¼ teaspoon onion powder
Black pepper, to taste

Carrot and Ginger Soup:

3 tablespoons olive oil
4 cloves garlic, minced
2 stalks celery, diced
1 onion, minced
1 tablespoon chopped fresh ginger
3 large carrots, peeled and diced
3 yellow-fleshed potatoes (about 15 oz/425 g), peeled and diced
1 sweet potato (about 14 oz/400 g), peeled and diced
1 can (14 oz/398 mL) coconut milk
6 cups (1.5 L) vegetable broth
½ cup (70 g) cashews
3 tablespoons tomato paste
2 teaspoons sambal oelek
1½ teaspoons salt
¼ teaspoon ground turmeric
Black pepper, to taste

For the Chive and Lime Cream:

1. In a bowl, combine all the cream ingredients. Cover and refrigerate for up to 4 hours.

For the Carrot and Ginger Soup:

2. In a large pot over medium heat, heat the oil, then add the garlic, celery, onions, and ginger, and cook, stirring, for 5 minutes. Stir in the remaining soup ingredients and bring to a boil, then lower the heat and simmer for 45 minutes.

3. Using an immersion blender in the pot, or transferring the soup to a blender, blend the soup until smooth.

4. Divide the soup among six bowls, garnish with the chive and lime cream, and serve. Leftover soup can be stored in the fridge in an airtight container for up to 4 days. Reheat in a saucepan over medium heat for about 5 minutes, or until hot.

Mains

Impossible Meatballs with Diabolo Sauce

Serves 4 | Prep Time: 40 min | Chill Time: 20 min | Cook Time: 35 min

When I was a kid, my mom often made her famous meatballs in Fra Diavolo sauce. I recently asked my mom for that recipe, and she miraculously had it on hand. Do moms ever throw anything away? I used my mom's recipe as a starting point and created my own version of the popular sweet-and-sour meatballs—making them vegan, of course. This recipe is at its best when made with the Impossible Burger brand of plant-based meat.

Meatballs:

½ cup (90 g) long-grain white rice, rinsed

1 cup (250 mL) water

3 tablespoons vegetable oil (approx.)

1 onion, minced

1 package (12 oz/340 g) plant-based ground meat, such as Impossible Burger

¼ cup (27 g) breadcrumbs

1 teaspoon sweet paprika

1 teaspoon ground cumin

1 teaspoon salt

½ teaspoon dried thyme

Black pepper, to taste

Diabolo Sauce:

1 tablespoon vegetable oil

1 onion, minced

1 cup (250 mL) ketchup

⅔ cup (160 mL) vegetable broth

½ cup (125 mL) chili sauce, such as Heinz

¼ cup (55 g) packed brown sugar

1 tablespoon vegan Worcestershire sauce

½ teaspoon mustard powder

¼ teaspoon red pepper flakes

For the Meatballs:

1. Place the rice in a heavy-bottomed saucepan, then add the water. Bring to a boil, then lower the heat to the minimum, cover, and simmer for 10 minutes.

2. Remove from the heat and let rest, covered, for 15 minutes.

3. Meanwhile, in a skillet over medium heat, heat the oil, then add the onion and cook, stirring, for 5 minutes.

4. Using a slotted spoon, transfer the cooked onion to a large bowl, leaving any remaining oil in the pan. Add the cooked rice and the remaining meatball ingredients to the cooked onion. Use your hands to thoroughly combine.

5. Use a ¼-cup (60 mL) ice-cream scoop to shape 12 meatballs. Transfer to a tray and refrigerate for 20 minutes.

6. In the skillet you used to cook the onions, cook the meatballs over medium heat for 15 minutes, turning until browned on all sides, adding more oil to the pan if needed. Transfer to a plate and set aside.

For the Diabolo Sauce:

7. In a skillet over medium heat, heat the oil, then add the onion and cook, stirring, for 5 minutes. Add the remaining sauce ingredients and cook for 5 minutes.

8. Stir the meatballs into the sauce and cook for 3 minutes, or until warmed through.

Cabbage Rolls

Serves 4 | Prep Time: 45 min | Cook Time: 45 min

I swear each culture has its own stuffed cabbage recipe. As a vegan, I couldn't be more thankful for this! What's better than a little bundle of cabbage and savory, tender filling bathed in a tangy sauce? To create my version, I took inspiration from the traditional Quebecois cabbage rolls I grew up with, and added a lot of my favorite flavors, like ginger, soy sauce, and hoisin sauce. The result blew me away! I hope you'll love it too.

Cabbage Rolls:

8 napa cabbage leaves
2 tablespoons olive oil
3 carrots, grated
2 stalks celery, diced
1 onion, minced
3 cloves garlic, minced
1 tablespoon minced fresh ginger
1 package (12 oz/340 g) plant-based ground meat, such as Impossible Burger
1 cup (250 mL) cooked basmati rice (page 167)
¼ cup (60 mL) hoisin sauce
1 teaspoon salt

Sauce:

¼ cup (60 mL) soy sauce
¼ cup (60 mL) maple syrup
¼ cup (60 mL) vegetable broth
4 green onions, minced
4 cloves garlic, minced
¼ teaspoon ground allspice
¼ teaspoon red pepper flakes

For the Cabbage Rolls:

1. Preheat the oven to 400°F (200°C).

2. Fill a pot with water and bring to a boil. Add the cabbage leaves and blanch for 1 minute. Drain and set aside.

3. In a skillet over medium heat, heat the oil, then add the carrots, celery, onion, garlic, and ginger, and cook, stirring, for 5 minutes.

4. Add the plant-based meat and cook for 5 minutes, breaking it apart with a wooden spoon, until light golden brown.

5. Stir in the rice, hoisin sauce, and salt. Remove from the heat and let cool for a few minutes.

6. Divide the filling among the cabbage leaves (about ½ cup/125 mL per leaf). Fold the long sides of the cabbage leaf over the filling, then roll from one short end to the other to seal like a spring roll. Transfer the stuffed cabbage leaves to a 9 × 13-inch (23 × 33 cm) baking dish, seam side down.

For the Sauce:

7. In a small saucepan, combine all the sauce ingredients. Bring to a boil, then lower the heat and simmer for 5 minutes.

8. Pour the sauce over the cabbage rolls and bake for 30 minutes.

Impossible Tacos

Makes 12 tacos | Prep Time: 30 min | Cook Time: 15 min

Thanks to the arrival of plant-based meat, cooking a quick vegan lunch from scratch is becoming easier and easier. In this recipe, I use plant-based meat to create flavorful tacos that will please carnivores and vegans alike. These tacos are filled with flavor and spices, and they're super-quick to prepare. You start by sautéing the plant-based meat with spices, then divide it among taco shells. Garnish with vegan sour cream and you're done!

Pico de Gallo:

2 tomatoes, diced

¼ red onion, minced

¼ cup (15 g) minced fresh cilantro (optional)

Juice from ½ lime

Salt and black pepper, to taste

Vegan Sour Cream:

2 green onions, minced

⅓ cup (80 mL) vegan mayonnaise

¼ cup (60 mL) soy cream

Juice from ½ lime

1 tablespoon maple syrup

1 teaspoon garlic powder

1 teaspoon onion powder

½ teaspoon salt

Black pepper, to taste

For the Pico de Gallo:

1. In a bowl, combine the tomatoes, red onion, cilantro (if using), and lime juice. Season with salt and pepper. Set aside.

For the Vegan Sour Cream:

2. In a bowl, whisk together all the sour cream ingredients. Set aside.

Recipe continues

Filling:

3 tablespoons vegetable oil

1 onion, minced

1 red bell pepper, diced

1 jalapeño pepper, seeded and minced

8 ounces (225 g) white button mushrooms, chopped

1 package (12 oz/340 g) plant-based ground meat, such as Impossible Burger

2 tablespoons nutritional yeast

1 tablespoon chili powder

2 teaspoons maple syrup

1 teaspoon salt

Black pepper, to taste

To Serve:

12 hard taco shells

2 cups (100 g) minced iceberg lettuce

For the Filling:

3. In a large skillet over medium-high heat, heat the oil, then add the onion, bell pepper, jalapeño, and mushrooms, and cook, stirring, for 10 minutes.

4. Add the plant-based meat and cook for 5 minutes, breaking it apart with a wooden spoon, until light golden brown.

5. Add the remaining filling ingredients and cook, stirring, for 1 minute.

To Serve:

6. Divide the filling among the taco shells. Garnish with pico de gallo, vegan sour cream, and lettuce.

Sweet Potato Enchiladas

Serves 3 | Prep Time: 30 min | Cook Time: 1 hour

I love Tex-Mex and other diasporic Mexican cuisines because they often showcase legumes in delicious dishes like tacos, burritos, salsas, and salads. One of my favorite dishes is enchiladas. I've added sweet potato to these enchiladas, as it imparts a really lovely sweet touch. The delicious, no-cook sauce is so easy to make. Simply stir all the ingredients together, add it to the enchiladas, bake, and enjoy!

Filling:

3 tablespoons olive oil

1 onion, minced

1 red bell pepper, finely chopped

1 sweet potato (about 14 oz/400 g), peeled and finely diced

8 ounces (225 g) white button mushrooms, finely chopped

1 teaspoon salt

1 can (14 oz/398 mL) black beans, rinsed and drained

1 cup (250 mL) vegetable broth

1 tablespoon chili powder

1 tablespoon maple syrup

1 teaspoon smoked paprika

Sauce:

1 jar (24 oz/700 mL) tomato passata

¾ cup (180 mL) vegetable broth

1 tablespoon chili powder

1 teaspoon dried oregano

1 teaspoon instant coffee granules

1 teaspoon salt

¼ teaspoon cayenne pepper

Black pepper, to taste

3 tablespoons maple syrup

For the Filling:

1. In a skillet over medium-high heat, heat the oil, then add the onion, bell pepper, sweet potato, mushrooms, and salt, and cook for 15 minutes, stirring frequently.

2. Stir in the remaining filling ingredients and cook until the liquid is fully absorbed, about 12 minutes.

3. Transfer the mixture to a bowl and refrigerate while you prepare the sauce.

For the Sauce:

4. In a bowl, combine all the sauce ingredients.

Recipe continues

To Assemble:

6 small tortillas

2½ cups (225 g) grated vegan cheese

To Assemble:

5. Preheat the oven to 375°F (190°C).

6. Spread half of the sauce in the bottom of an 8 × 11-inch (20 × 28 cm) baking dish.

7. Place ½ cup (125 mL) of the filling in the center of each tortilla. Roll up the tortillas and nestle into the sauce, seam side down. Pour the remaining sauce over the tortillas. Sprinkle with vegan cheese.

8. Bake for 30 minutes, or until the cheese is melted and beginning to brown.

Veggie Pâté Hand Pies

Makes 16 pies | Prep Time: 25 min | Cook Time: 25 min

We hosted a dinner in our new house and, out of all my recipes, this is the one I made for our guests. When you're a vegan, you can't afford to disappoint guests, because they're so few and far between . . . Well, mission accomplished! My guests loved these hand pies. This versatile recipe can be served for lunch or an elegant dinner, or packed up and taken to the office.

Veggie Pâté (page 14)
12 sheets phyllo pastry
Vegetable oil, for brushing
2 cups (35 g) baby spinach
Arrabbiata Sauce (below)

1. Preheat the oven to 375°F (190°C). Line a baking sheet with parchment paper.

2. Slice the veggie pâté widthwise into 4 pieces, then slice each piece in half lengthwise to produce 8 rectangles. Slice each rectangle on the diagonal to produce 16 triangles.

3. Place 1 sheet of phyllo pastry on a clean work surface. Lightly brush with oil all over. Top with a second sheet, brush with oil, then add a third sheet and brush with oil again. Repeat three times with the remaining phyllo sheets to create 4 separate stacks of phyllo.

4. Using a sharp knife or kitchen shears, cut each phyllo stack widthwise into 4 pieces.

5. Along a short edge of each phyllo rectangle, place about 10 leaves of baby spinach and top with 1 triangle of veggie pâté. Fold one corner of the pastry over the filling. Keep folding the pastry, as you would a flag, to create a triangular hand pie. Repeat with the remaining pastry.

6. Transfer the prepared hand pies to the prepared baking sheet and brush with oil.

7. Bake for 20 to 25 minutes, or until the pies are crisp and golden brown.

8. Serve warm with arrabbiata sauce for dipping.

Recipe continues

ARRABBIATA SAUCE
Makes 3 cups (750 mL) | Prep Time: 15 min | Cook Time: 40 min

1 jar (12 oz/340 mL) roasted red
  bell peppers, drained and rinsed
3 tablespoons olive oil
1 onion, minced
5 cloves garlic, minced
1 can (28 oz/796 mL) diced
  tomatoes, with juice
2 bay leaves
2 tablespoons cane sugar
2 teaspoons dried oregano
1 teaspoon dried basil
1 teaspoon salt
½ teaspoon red pepper flakes
Black pepper, to taste

1. In a blender, blend the roasted red peppers until smooth. Set aside.

2. In a large pot over medium heat, heat the oil, then add the onion and cook, stirring, for 5 minutes. Add the garlic and cook, stirring, for 2 minutes.

3. Add the blended peppers and the remaining ingredients, and bring to a boil. Lower the heat and simmer for 30 minutes, stirring regularly. Remove the bay leaves before serving. Sauce can be stored in an airtight container in the fridge for up to 4 days.

Mushroom Stroganoff

Serves 4 | Prep Time: 40 min | Cook Time: 30 min

I'm not sure who this Stroganoff person was, but they made darn good recipes. Especially this one, which I've transformed into a vegan version by replacing the beef with mushrooms. I think the mushrooms make this recipe even better than the original!

Mushroom Stroganoff:

3 tablespoons olive oil

1 onion, minced

14 ounces (400 g) king oyster mushrooms, sliced into rounds

8 ounces (225 g) white button mushrooms

1½ teaspoons salt

3 cloves garlic, minced

½ cup (125 mL) white wine

¼ cup (32 g) all-purpose flour

1¼ cups (310 mL) vegetable broth

1 cup (250 mL) soy cream

2 tablespoons nutritional yeast

1 tablespoon sweet paprika

1 teaspoon smoked paprika

¼ teaspoon dried thyme

⅛ teaspoon cayenne pepper

Black pepper, to taste

3 tablespoons maple syrup

2 tablespoons tomato paste

1 tablespoon whole-grain mustard

1 tablespoon lemon juice

For the Mushroom Stroganoff:

1. In a large pot over medium-high heat, heat the oil, then add the onion, oyster and button mushrooms, and salt, and cook, stirring frequently, for 12 to 15 minutes, or until the vegetables are soft. Add the garlic and wine, and simmer until the liquid is fully evaporated.

2. Add the flour and stir until combined. Gradually whisk in the broth and soy cream. Stir in the remaining stroganoff ingredients and bring to a boil, then lower the heat and simmer for 12 minutes. Keep warm on low heat until ready to serve.

Recipe continues

Garlic Butter Tagliatelle:

10½ ounces (300 g) dried tagliatelle pasta

¼ cup (60 mL) vegan butter, such as Earth Balance

4 cloves garlic, minced

2 tablespoons nutritional yeast

¾ teaspoon salt

Black pepper, to taste

1 tablespoon lemon juice

⅓ cup (20 g) fresh parsley, minced

For the Garlic Butter Tagliatelle:

3. Meanwhile, cook the pasta according to the package directions. Drain, reserving ¾ cup (180 mL) of the pasta cooking water.

4. In a saucepan over medium heat, melt the vegan butter. Add the garlic and cook for 3 minutes, stirring frequently. Stir in the yeast, salt, and pepper. Stir in the cooked pasta, lemon juice, and pasta cooking water, and cook until the liquid is fully absorbed. Stir in the parsley and season to taste.

5. Transfer the pasta to a serving platter and top with the stroganoff.

Italian Sausage Macaroni

Serves 6 | Prep Time: 15 min | Cook Time: 20 min

I was missing the macaroni dish my mom used to make when I was a kid, so I recreated her recipe using vegan sausages. The result was this extraordinary macaroni that may be even better than my mom's (but don't tell her I said that)!

2 tablespoons olive oil

3 cloves garlic, minced

1 onion, minced

4 vegan sausages

1 can (28 oz/796 mL) diced tomatoes, with juice

1 tablespoon dried basil

1 tablespoon dried oregano

1 teaspoon salt

¼ teaspoon red pepper flakes

2 tablespoons maple syrup

12½ ounces (355 g) dried macaroni pasta

1. In a large pot over medium heat, heat the oil, then add the garlic and onion, and cook, stirring, for 5 minutes. Add the sausages and cook for 5 minutes, breaking them apart with a spatula.

2. Stir in the tomatoes, basil, oregano, salt, red pepper flakes, and maple syrup, and cook for 10 minutes.

3. Meanwhile, cook the pasta according to the package directions. Drain.

4. Add the pasta to the sauce and stir to combine.

Vegan Paella with Sausage

Serves 6 | Prep Time: 40 min | Cook Time: 65 min

New varieties of plant-based meats are constantly appearing on grocery store shelves. Vegan sausages are one of my favorite products so far! Plant-based meat is practical, fast, and delicious. In short, "it does the job," as my father used to say. In this paella recipe, I also add nori, the type of seaweed used to make sushi. Along with the vegan sausage, it creates the surf 'n' turf flavor that makes paella so delicious.

6 tablespoons (90 mL) vegetable oil, divided

4 spicy vegan sausages

2 portobello mushrooms, thinly sliced

1 large onion, minced

1 orange bell pepper, diced

1 can (14 oz/398 mL) hearts of palm, drained, rinsed, and sliced into rounds

5 cloves garlic, minced

1 sheet nori, minced

½ cup (125 mL) dry white wine

2½ cups (625 mL) vegetable broth

1 can (28 oz/796 mL) diced tomatoes, with juice

1½ cups (270 g) long-grain white rice, rinsed

¼ cup (15 g) nutritional yeast

2 tablespoons maple syrup

2 teaspoons smoked paprika

2 teaspoons salt

1 teaspoon dried oregano

1 teaspoon dried basil

½ teaspoon dried thyme

¼ teaspoon ground turmeric

¼ teaspoon cayenne pepper

1 generous pinch saffron threads

Lemon wedges, for garnish

Chopped fresh parsley, for garnish

1. Preheat the oven to 375°F (190°C).

2. In a large pot over medium-high heat, heat half of the oil. Add the sausages and cook for 8 minutes, flipping halfway through. Remove the sausages from the pot, slice into rounds, and set aside.

3. In the same pot, heat the remaining oil, then add the mushrooms, onion, and bell pepper, and cook for 8 minutes, stirring frequently. Stir in the hearts of palm, garlic, and nori, and cook for 2 minutes. Add the wine, bring to a boil and cook for 1 minute.

4. Stir in the remaining ingredients, except the reserved sausages and the garnishes, and return to a boil. Transfer the mixture to a 10 x 15-inch (25 x 38 cm) baking dish.

5. Bake for 25 minutes. Arrange the sausage rounds over the paella and bake for 15 minutes.

6. Garnish with lemon wedges and parsley.

Sausage and Mushroom Rice

Serves 4 | Prep Time: 40 min | Cook Time: 30 min | Rest Time: 15 min

Let's be honest . . . rice can be boring, right? But it's so easy to inject flavor into white rice that there's never an excuse for eating a boring rice dish. This recipe combines earthy mushrooms, savory garlic, white wine, vegan Italian sausages, and vegetable broth for a simple yet flavorful dish. You've got to give it a try! I promise it's not boring.

5 tablespoons (75 mL) olive oil, divided

4 vegan Italian sausages

1 onion, minced

8 ounces (225 g) white button mushrooms, chopped

½ cup (125 mL) white wine

6 cups (105 g) baby spinach

2½ cups (625 mL) vegetable broth

1½ cups (270 g) jasmine rice, rinsed

½ cup (125 mL) soy cream

2 cloves garlic, minced

3 tablespoons nutritional yeast

1 teaspoon salt

1 teaspoon dried herbes de Provence

½ teaspoon mustard powder

Black pepper, to taste

1 tablespoon maple syrup

1 teaspoon truffle oil (optional)

1. In a large pot over medium-high heat, heat 2 tablespoons of the oil. Add the sausages and cook for 8 minutes, turning them frequently. Remove the sausages from the pot, slice into rounds, and set aside.

2. In the same pot over medium-high heat, heat the remaining oil, then add the onion and mushrooms, and sauté for 5 minutes. Add the wine and reduce for 2 minutes.

3. Add the remaining ingredients, except the reserved sausages, and stir to combine.

4. Set the sausage rounds over the rice mixture and bring to a boil, then lower the heat, cover, and simmer for 10 to 12 minutes, or until the liquid is fully absorbed.

5. Remove from the heat and let rest, covered, for 15 minutes.

Vegan Fried Chicken

Serves 4 | Prep Time: 20 min | Cook Time: 15 min

This is the absolute best vegan fried "chicken," juicy and tender on the inside but super crunchy on the outside. Just like your favorite fast-food chicken, except that it's made with . . . oyster mushrooms. You'll go crazy for it!

Ranch Mayonnaise:

½ cup (125 mL) vegan mayonnaise
3 tablespoons minced chives
1½ teaspoons onion powder
½ teaspoon garlic powder
¼ teaspoon salt
Black pepper, to taste
2 tablespoons soy cream
2 teaspoons apple cider vinegar
1½ teaspoons maple syrup

Vegan Fried Chicken:

Vegetable oil, for frying
2¼ cups (260 g) spelt flour, divided
1 teaspoon onion powder
1 teaspoon garlic powder
1 teaspoon salt
1 cup (250 mL) unsweetened soy milk
1 tablespoon maple syrup
1 teaspoon smoked paprika
½ teaspoon dried thyme
¼ teaspoon ground sage
¼ teaspoon cayenne pepper
Black pepper, to taste
10 ounces (280 g) oyster mushrooms

For the Ranch Mayonnaise:

1. In a bowl, whisk all the mayonnaise ingredients to a smooth consistency. Mayonnaise will keep in an airtight container in the fridge for up to 4 days.

For the Vegan Fried Chicken:

2. In a deep fryer or a deep pot, preheat 3 inches (8 cm) of oil to 350°F (180°C).

3. In a bowl, whisk together 1¼ cups (145 g) of the flour with the onion powder, garlic powder, salt, soy milk, and maple syrup.

4. In a second bowl, whisk together the remaining flour with the paprika, thyme, sage, cayenne pepper, and black pepper.

5. Dip each mushroom in the wet batter, then roll in the dry breading and place on a plate.

6. Drop the breaded mushrooms into the hot oil, 2 at a time. Fry until golden brown, about 3 to 4 minutes, then transfer to a paper towel–lined plate. Repeat to fry all the mushrooms.

7. Serve with the Ranch Mayonnaise.

Mushroom Linguine

Serves 4 | Prep Time: 45 min | Cook Time: 15 min

The delicate aroma of white wine, the nutty flavor of mushrooms, and the creamy texture of cashew sauce—combined, these ingredients create the ultimate comfort dish. The robust flavors of this satisfying dish will please even the pickiest palates.

Cashew Cream:

1 cup (140 g) cashews
2 cups (500 mL) vegetable broth
⅓ cup (20 g) nutritional yeast
1 teaspoon dried basil
1 teaspoon dried oregano
1 teaspoon garlic powder
1 teaspoon salt
¼ teaspoon red pepper flakes
Black pepper, to taste
2 teaspoons apple cider vinegar
2 teaspoons maple syrup
½ teaspoon truffle oil (optional)

Sautéed Mushrooms:

3 tablespoons olive oil
8 ounces (225 g) white button
    mushrooms, chopped
2 portobello mushrooms, chopped
1 onion, minced
8 cups (140 g) baby spinach
4 cloves garlic, minced
¼ teaspoon salt
⅓ cup (80 mL) white wine

Linguine:

11½ ounces (325 g) dried linguine
    pasta

For the Cashew Cream:

1. Soak the cashews in boiling water for 15 minutes. Drain.

2. Add the soaked cashews and the remaining cashew cream ingredients to a blender and blend until smooth. Set aside.

For the Sautéed Mushrooms:

3. In a skillet over medium-high heat, heat the oil, then add the button mushrooms, portobello mushrooms, and onion, and cook, stirring, for 10 minutes. Gradually stir in the spinach. Add the garlic and salt, and cook for 3 minutes, stirring frequently. Add the wine and simmer for 2 minutes. Stir in the cashew cream.

For the Linguine:

4. Meanwhile, cook the pasta according to the package directions. Drain.

5. Add the pasta to the sautéed mushrooms and stir to coat the pasta with the sauce.

Creamy Squash Fusilli

Serves 4 | Prep Time: 35 min | Cook Time: 20 min

Squash are magnificent. They exist in all shapes and sizes. Unfortunately, we often put them in our grocery carts, then come home and ask ourselves, "What will I ever do with this squash?" My secret is roasting them in the oven. This caramelizes their flesh, wakes up their flavor, and makes them even sweeter.

Butternut Squash:

1 butternut squash (about 2 lbs/ 900 g), peeled, seeded, and cut into small dice
3 tablespoons olive oil
¼ teaspoon salt
¼ teaspoon sweet paprika
Black pepper, to taste

Cashew Béchamel:

⅔ cup (95 g) cashews
2 cups (500 mL) vegetable broth
½ cup (30 g) nutritional yeast
¼ cup (60 mL) vegetable oil
2 tablespoons cornstarch
1 tablespoon maple syrup
1 teaspoon salt
2 teaspoons apple cider vinegar
1 teaspoon truffle oil (optional)

Fusilli:

12½ ounces (355 g) dried fusilli pasta

For the Butternut Squash:

1. Preheat the oven to 400°F (200°C).

2. In a bowl, combine the squash, oil, salt, paprika, and pepper, tossing to coat. Transfer to a baking sheet and spread out in a single layer.

3. Roast for 20 minutes, or until the squash is tender, tossing halfway through.

For the Cashew Béchamel and the Fusilli:

4. Meanwhile, soak the cashews in boiling water for 15 minutes. Drain.

5. While the cashews are soaking, cook the pasta according to the package directions. Drain and set aside.

6. Add the soaked cashews and the remaining béchamel ingredients to a blender and blend until smooth.

7. Pour the cashew sauce into a saucepan and bring to a simmer over medium heat, whisking constantly. When the sauce simmers, lower the heat and cook for 1 minute, stirring constantly.

8. Add the squash to the cashew béchamel and stir to combine. Add the pasta and toss to coat with the sauce.

Tagliatelle with Creamy Sun-Dried Tomato Pesto

Serves 4 | Prep Time: 30 min | Cook Time: 30 min

If you like tomatoes, then you'll love this recipe. Not only are there oven-roasted cherry tomatoes, but there is also a sun-dried tomato, garlic, and basil pesto. This style of pesto, often called pesto rosso, is super flavorful and naturally sweet. Another thing I love about this recipe is that it makes for excellent leftovers. Simply reheat it for lunch the next day!

Roasted Tomatoes:

1 shallot, minced

2 tablespoons olive oil

1 tablespoon balsamic vinegar

1 teaspoon garlic powder

¼ teaspoon salt

Black pepper, to taste

2 cups (300 g) cherry tomatoes

3 tablespoons chopped fresh basil

Tagliatelle:

12½ ounces (355 g) dried tagliatelle pasta

Sun-Dried Tomato Pesto:

4 cups (240 g) loosely packed fresh basil leaves

¾ cup (105 g) cashews

½ cup (30 g) nutritional yeast

⅓ cup (80 mL) olive oil

¼ cup + ⅔ cup (220 mL) water, divided

10 sun-dried tomatoes

3 cloves garlic, minced

1 teaspoon salt

Black pepper, to taste

2 teaspoons maple syrup

1 cup (250 mL) soy cream

For the Roasted Tomatoes:

1. Preheat the oven to 400°F (200°C). Grease a baking sheet with oil.

2. In a bowl, combine the shallot, oil, vinegar, garlic powder, salt, and pepper. Add the cherry tomatoes and toss to coat. Transfer to the prepared baking sheet and spread out in a single layer.

3. Bake for 20 minutes, tossing halfway through. Add the chopped basil and stir to combine.

For the Tagliatelle:

4. Meanwhile, cook the pasta according to the package directions. Drain and set aside.

For the Sun-Dried Tomato Pesto:

5. In a food processor, combine the basil, cashews, yeast, oil, ¼ cup (60 mL) water, sun-dried tomatoes, garlic, salt, pepper, and maple syrup, and process until smooth.

6. Pour the basil mixture into a skillet over medium heat and cook for 3 minutes, stirring frequently. Add the soy cream and ⅔ cup (160 mL) water. Bring to a boil, then lower the heat and simmer for 1 minute.

7. Add the cooked pasta, turn the heat to low, and cook for 2 minutes, stirring continuously.

8. Serve garnished with the roasted tomatoes.

Vegan Salisbury Steak

Serves 5 | Prep Time: 50 min | Cook Time: 50 min

I had a craving for simple and satisfying old-school, stick-to-your-ribs comfort food, so I created this vegan Salisbury steak. The combination of mushrooms, lentils, and spices creates a texture that's almost identical to a ground beef patty that would traditionally be used in Salisbury steak. The creamy, aromatic sauce has a slightly smoky flavor, which perfectly complements the vegan steak.

Salisbury Steak:

2 portobello mushrooms

1 onion, quartered

3 tablespoons olive oil

1 can (14 oz/398 mL) brown lentils, rinsed and drained

¼ cup (15 g) nutritional yeast

¼ cup (60 mL) chili sauce, such as Heinz

¼ cup (60 mL) soy sauce

1 tablespoon maple syrup

1 teaspoon sweet paprika

1 teaspoon garlic powder

½ teaspoon mustard powder

¾ cup (90 g) all-purpose flour

¾ cup (80 g) breadcrumbs

For the Salisbury Steak:

1. Preheat the oven to 375°F (190°C). Grease a baking sheet with oil.

2. Using a food processor or a knife, coarsely slice the mushrooms and onion.

3. In a skillet over medium heat, heat the oil, then add the mushrooms and onion, and cook for 4 minutes, stirring frequently. Stir in the remaining steak ingredients, except the flour and breadcrumbs, and cook for 2 minutes.

4. Transfer the mixture to a large bowl, then stir in the flour and breadcrumbs. Divide the mixture into 5 patties (about 5 oz/150 g each) and place the patties on the prepared baking sheet.

5. Bake for 30 minutes, or until lightly browned.

Recipe continues

Sauce:

3 tablespoons olive oil

2 onions, minced

8 ounces (225 g) white button mushrooms, finely chopped

½ cup (125 mL) white wine

2½ cups (625 mL) vegetable broth

¼ cup (60 mL) miso paste

¼ cup (60 mL) ketchup

1 tablespoon vegan Worcestershire sauce

1 tablespoon maple syrup

1 tablespoon maple syrup

2 teaspoons liquid smoke

Black pepper, to taste

1 tablespoon cornstarch mixed with 2 tablespoons water

To Serve:

Baked Baby Potatoes (page 139)

For the Sauce:

6. In a skillet over medium heat, heat the oil, then add the onions and mushrooms, and cook, stirring, for 5 minutes. Add the wine and cook for 2 minutes.

7. Stir in the remaining sauce ingredients, except the cornstarch mixture. Bring to a boil, then lower the heat and simmer for 5 minutes.

8. Stir in the cornstarch mixture and bring to a boil, stirring constantly.

To Serve:

9. Nestle the patties into the sauce and serve with the baked baby potatoes. .

Chickpea Stew with Fragrant Rice

Serves 4 to 6 | Prep Time: 30 min | Cook Time: 25 min

I love chickpeas. As a rich source of vitamins, minerals, and fiber, they offer a variety of health benefits, such as improving digestion and reducing your risk of disease. But above all else, they're delicious! I like adding them to simple yet incredibly satisfying stews like this one. It's served with fragrant rice and pita chips, both of which are also tasty on their own.

Fragrant Rice:

3 tablespoons olive oil
4 cloves garlic, minced
1 shallot, minced
2 cups (500 mL) vegetable broth
1 cup (180 g) jasmine rice, rinsed
1 teaspoon dried oregano
½ teaspoon cumin seeds
¼ teaspoon ground turmeric
1 tablespoon tomato paste
1 teaspoon maple syrup
1 teaspoon harissa sauce
1 teaspoon lemon juice

Chickpea Stew:

¼ cup (60 mL) olive oil
2 onions, minced
1¼ teaspoons salt
1 can (14 oz/398 mL) chickpeas, rinsed and drained
1¼ cups (165 g) frozen green peas
2 cloves garlic, minced
16 cups (280 g) baby spinach
½ cup (125 mL) vegetable broth
½ cup (125 mL) soy cream

For the Fragrant Rice:

1. In a large pot over medium heat, heat the oil, then add the garlic and shallot, and cook, stirring, for 2 minutes.

2. Stir in the remaining ingredients and bring to a boil, then lower the heat and simmer for 10 minutes, or until the liquid is fully absorbed.

3. Remove from the heat and let rest, covered, for 10 minutes. Stir before serving.

For the Chickpea Stew:

4. Meanwhile, in another large pot over medium heat, heat the oil, then add the onions and salt, and cook, stirring, for 5 minutes. Stir in the chickpeas, green peas, and garlic, and cook for 8 minutes, gradually stirring in the spinach.

5. Stir in the remaining ingredients and bring to a boil, then lower the heat and simmer for 4 minutes, stirring frequently.

For the Pita Chips:

6. Meanwhile, in a skillet over medium heat, heat the oil, then add the pita slices and fry until golden brown, about 10 minutes, stirring from time to time, and adding more oil as needed.

7. Sprinkle the pita chips with yeast, garlic powder, paprika, and salt, and toss to distribute the seasonings.

Recipe continues

2 teaspoons ground sumac
¼ teaspoon red pepper flakes
Black pepper, to taste
2 teaspoons maple syrup
1 teaspoon lemon juice

Pita Chips:

3 tablespoons olive oil (approx.)
2 small pita breads, each cut into
    12 slices
2 tablespoons nutritional yeast
½ teaspoon garlic powder
¼ teaspoon sweet paprika
Pinch of salt

To Serve:

8. Serve the stew over the rice and garnish with the pita chips.

Lentil Stew Cigars

Serves 4 | Prep Time: 45 min | Chill Time: 20 min | Cook Time: 45 min

Phyllo pastry (also spelled filo pastry) is a very thin, flaky pastry used in Mediterranean cooking. It must be handled with care because it's very delicate. To use it, you stack several sheets, brushing each one with oil. The result is a super-light and flaky pastry that you can use in both savory and sweet recipes. In this recipe, the meaty texture of the filling against the crispy phyllo pastry will surprise even die-hard carnivores.

3 tablespoons olive oil

8 ounces (225 g) white button mushrooms, finely chopped

4 cloves garlic, minced

1 onion, minced

1 red bell pepper, diced

¾ cup (105 g) cashews, coarsely chopped

1 tablespoon grated fresh ginger

1 teaspoon salt

1 can (14 oz/398 mL) brown lentils, rinsed and drained

1 cup (250 mL) vegetable broth

¼ cup (15 g) nutritional yeast

1 tablespoon soy sauce

1 tablespoon maple syrup

¼ teaspoon red pepper flakes

¼ teaspoon ground allspice

¼ teaspoon dried thyme

Black pepper, to taste

¾ cup (80 g) breadcrumbs

9 sheets phyllo pastry

½ cup (125 mL) vegetable oil (approx.)

1. In a skillet over medium-high heat, heat the olive oil, then add the mushrooms, garlic, onion, bell pepper, cashews, ginger, and salt, and cook for 8 minutes, stirring frequently.

2. Stir in the lentils, broth, yeast, soy sauce, maple syrup, red pepper flakes, allspice, thyme, and black pepper. Bring to a boil, then lower the heat to medium and cook for 5 minutes, stirring frequently, until half of the liquid is absorbed. Remove from the heat and stir in the breadcrumbs.

3. Transfer the mixture to a bowl and refrigerate for about 20 minutes.

4. Preheat the oven to 375°F (190°C). Grease a baking sheet with oil.

5. Place 1 sheet of phyllo pastry on a clean work surface. Lightly brush with vegetable oil all over. Top with a second sheet, brush with oil, then add a third sheet and brush with oil again. Repeat three times with the remaining phyllo sheets to create 3 separate stacks of phyllo.

6. Using a sharp knife or kitchen shears, cut each phyllo stack in half widthwise, then in half lengthwise, to produce 4 rectangles.

7. Along a short edge of each phyllo rectangle, spoon about ½ cup (125 mL) of the lentil stew. Fold the long edges of the pastry over the stew, then roll the short end over the filling until it meets the other end, sealing the filling like a spring roll.

8. Transfer the lentil stew rolls to the prepared baking sheet. Lightly brush each roll with vegetable oil.

9. Bake for 30 minutes, or until the pastry is crispy and golden.

Vegan Lobster Rolls

Serves 4 | Prep Time: 20 min | Cook Time: 15 min | Chill Time: 20 min

Every summer, my wife and I rent a cabin in Gaspésie, in eastern Quebec. This region is renowned for its lobster, but we don't feel left out. While we're there, we make a point of preparing our famous vegan lobster rolls, which are made with chickpeas and hearts of palm. The mayonnaise itself is incredible, seasoned with just the right amount of dill and lime juice. It adds richness and creaminess to the filling.

Filling:

3 tablespoons olive oil

2 cans (14 oz/398 mL) hearts of palm, rinsed, drained, and sliced into half-rounds

1 can (14 oz/398 mL) chickpeas, rinsed and drained

2 stalks celery, diced

½ orange bell pepper, diced

¼ red onion, minced

½ cup (125 mL) vegetable broth

2 cloves garlic, minced

1 sheet nori, torn into small pieces

Seasoned Mayonnaise:

¾ cup (180 mL) vegan mayonnaise

3 tablespoons minced chives

2 teaspoons minced dill

1 teaspoon garlic powder

½ teaspoon sweet paprika

½ teaspoon salt

¼ teaspoon celery salt

¼ teaspoon red pepper flakes

Black pepper, to taste

1 tablespoon maple syrup

2 teaspoons lime juice

To Serve:

4 hot dog buns

For the Filling:

1. In a skillet over medium-high heat, heat the oil, then add the hearts of palm, chickpeas, celery, bell pepper, and onion, and cook, stirring, for 5 minutes. Stir in the remaining ingredients and cook, stirring frequently, until the vegetables are tender and the liquid is fully absorbed, about 8 to 10 minutes.

2. Transfer to a bowl and let cool completely, then refrigerate for 20 minutes.

For the Seasoned Mayonnaise:

3. In a bowl, whisk together all the mayonnaise ingredients.

To Serve:

4. Stir the seasoned mayonnaise into the filling. Divide the filling among the buns.

Mnazaleh (Braised Eggplant and Chickpeas)

Serves 6 | Prep Time: 30 min | Rest Time: 30 min | Cook Time: 55 min

Mnazaleh (pronounced *min-ah-zah-lay*) is an incredibly comforting dish that delivers rich Middle Eastern flavors. My secret trick (or not so secret now . . .) is to generously sprinkle the sliced eggplant with salt, then let it rest for 30 minutes before rinsing. The salt pulls excess water out of the eggplant, concentrating the flavor and helping it retain its texture and shape through cooking. The sweet raisins might be a surprising addition, but they make this recipe sing!

1 eggplant, cut into large cubes

1 tablespoon + 1 teaspoon salt, divided

3 tablespoons olive oil

2 onions, minced

1 can (28 oz/796 mL) diced tomatoes, with juice

1 can (14 oz/398 mL) chickpeas, rinsed and drained

1 cup (250 mL) vegetable broth

½ cup (65 g) raisins

1 teaspoon dried oregano

½ teaspoon ground cinnamon

½ teaspoon ground turmeric

½ teaspoon ground coriander

¼ teaspoon red pepper flakes

Black pepper, to taste

1 tablespoon maple syrup

1 teaspoon harissa sauce

1. Put the cubed eggplant in a sieve set over a bowl. Sprinkle with 1 tablespoon of salt and toss to combine. Let rest for 30 minutes.

2. Preheat the oven to 400°F (200°C).

3. Rinse the eggplant under cold running water to wash away the salt. Set aside.

4. In a skillet over medium heat, heat the oil, then add the onions and cook, stirring, for 5 minutes. Stir in the remaining 1 teaspoon salt, the eggplant, and the remaining ingredients, and bring to a boil. Transfer the mixture to an 8 × 11-inch (20 × 28 cm) baking dish.

5. Bake for 45 minutes, or until the mixture is bubbling rapidly.

Chana Masala

Serves 4 | Prep Time: 20 min | Cook Time: 30 min

I'm always looking for more ways to use my favorite legume: the chickpea! There are few chickpea recipes I've found better than chana masala, the popular Indian and Pakistani chickpea stew. In my rendition, I puree a third of the stew before mixing it back in, to create a lovely creamy texture.

2 tablespoons olive oil

1 onion, minced

1 tablespoon minced fresh ginger

2 cloves garlic, minced

1 can (28 oz/796 mL) diced tomatoes, with juice

1 can (19 oz/540 mL) chickpeas, rinsed and drained

1½ cups (375 mL) water

1 tablespoon curry powder

1 teaspoon cumin seeds

1 teaspoon salt

½ teaspoon ground coriander

¼ teaspoon red pepper flakes

Black pepper, to taste

1 tablespoon maple syrup

Chive and Lime Cream (page 71), for garnish

1. In a large saucepan over medium-high heat, heat the oil, then add the onion and cook, stirring, for 5 minutes. Add the ginger and garlic, and cook, stirring, for 2 minutes.

2. Stir in the remaining ingredients and bring to a boil, then lower the heat and simmer for 20 minutes.

3. Transfer a third of the mixture to a large measuring cup or a blender. Puree to a smooth consistency, using an immersion blender or the blender.

4. Pour the pureed mixture back into the saucepan and stir to combine.

5. Divide the stew among four bowls and garnish with the chive and lime cream right before serving.

Walnut Bolognese Sauce

Serves 12 | Prep Time: 40 min | Cook Time: 75 min

When people ask me how to decrease their meat consumption, I always give the same answer: veganize your favorite dishes. That's exactly what I did with this recipe. I made my mother's meat sauce vegan by replacing the beef with walnuts and tempeh, and it turned out fantastic. (Dare I say it tastes even better than the original?) Protein- and fiber-rich, this one-pot sauce is easy to prepare and incredibly flavorful.

2½ cups (350 g) walnuts, chopped

¼ cup (60 mL) olive oil

1 package (8½ oz/240 g) tempeh, finely chopped

5 cloves garlic, minced

3 carrots, grated

2 onions, minced

8 ounces (225 g) white button mushrooms, chopped

3 cans (each 28 oz/796 mL) diced tomatoes, with juice

1 can (5½ oz/156 mL) tomato paste

1 jar (12 oz/340 mL) roasted red bell peppers, drained, rinsed, and finely chopped

½ cup (110 g) packed brown sugar

⅓ cup (20 g) nutritional yeast

⅓ cup (80 mL) ketchup

1 tablespoon dried basil

1 tablespoon dried oregano

2 teaspoons salt

1 teaspoon dried thyme

1 teaspoon onion powder

1 teaspoon sweet paprika

1 teaspoon ground fenugreek

1 teaspoon ground cumin

½ teaspoon ground sage

½ teaspoon red pepper flakes

3 bay leaves

Black pepper, to taste

1. Preheat the oven to 400°F (200°C).

2. Spread the walnuts over a baking sheet. Toast in the oven for 5 to 6 minutes, watching constantly to make sure they don't burn. When lightly browned and fragrant, remove from the oven and set aside.

3. In a large pot over medium-high heat, heat the oil, then add the tempeh, garlic, carrots, onions, and mushrooms, and cook for 10 minutes, stirring frequently.

4. Stir in the toasted walnuts and the remaining ingredients, and bring to a boil, then lower the heat and simmer for 1 hour, stirring regularly.

5. Serve over the pasta of your choice. The cooled sauce will keep in airtight containers in the fridge for 5 days or in the freezer for 3 months.

Caramelized Onion Tempeh

Serves 3 to 4 | Prep Time: 45 min | Cook Time: 25 min

We don't all have the time or money to go to fancy restaurants. Not to worry, because I've provided this elegant recipe that will make you feel like you're out for a nice dinner. The secret to preparing tempeh properly is to gently poach it in broth to eliminate its bitterness. I also add maple syrup, liquid smoke, and Worcestershire sauce to the broth to inject even more flavor. Served over a creamy cauliflower and sweet potato puree, this dish is worthy of the finest china!

Caramelized Onion and Shiitake Sauce:

2 tablespoons olive oil

2 onions, minced

¼ teaspoon salt

4½ ounces (125 g) shiitake mushrooms, coarsely chopped

2 cloves garlic, minced

¼ cup (60 mL) water

2 teaspoons maple syrup

1 teaspoon balsamic vinegar

Black pepper, to taste

Cauliflower and Sweet Potato Puree:

4 cups (375 g) cauliflower florets

3 cloves garlic, peeled and smashed

2 sweet potatoes (about 1 lb/450 g), peeled and diced

2 tablespoons nutritional yeast

1 teaspoon onion powder

1 teaspoon garlic powder

1 teaspoon salt

1 teaspoon lemon juice

Black pepper, to taste

2 tablespoons soy cream

2 tablespoons vegan butter

For the Caramelized Onion and Shiitake Sauce:

1. In a skillet over medium heat, heat the oil, then add the onions and salt, and cook for 15 minutes, stirring frequently.

2. Stir in the remaining sauce ingredients and cook until the liquid is fully absorbed, about 8 minutes.

For the Cauliflower and Sweet Potato Puree:

3. Meanwhile, in a large pot of boiling water, boil the cauliflower, garlic, and sweet potatoes for 20 minutes, until tender, then drain.

4. Transfer to a bowl and add the remaining puree ingredients. Using an immersion blender or a potato masher, puree to a smooth consistency.

Recipe continues

Tempeh:

1 cup (250 mL) vegetable broth

3 tablespoons soy sauce

3 tablespoons maple syrup

2 tablespoons olive oil

1 teaspoon garlic powder

2 teaspoons vegan Worcestershire sauce

2 teaspoons lime juice

2 teaspoons hot sauce, such as Frank's RedHot

1½ teaspoons liquid smoke

1½ packages (each 8½ oz/240 g) tempeh

For the Tempeh:

5. While the sauce and vegetables are cooking, in a bowl, combine all the tempeh ingredients, except the tempeh. Set aside.

6. Slice the tempeh in half horizontally, then cut into triangles.

7. In another skillet over high heat, bring the tempeh and the broth mixture to a boil. Lower the heat and simmer until three-quarters of the liquid has evaporated, about 10 minutes.

To Serve:

8. On each serving plate, spoon a nest of puree. Top with some of the sauce and finish with a few slices of tempeh.

Buffalo Tofu Wraps

Serves 4 | Prep Time: 35 min | Chill Time: 1 hour | Cook Time: 10 min

I love wraps, but vegan wraps often leave me wanting more. I've tried so many versions—some with chickpeas, others with a ton of veggies—but they never lived up to my expectations. Then I tried using fried tofu. Wow! That was a game changer. In this recipe, crispy tofu is tossed with spicy Buffalo sauce and served in a wrap with aïoli and homemade slaw. You will be shocked by how hearty and flavorful these are!

Apple Slaw:

½ cup (125 mL) soy cream
½ cup (125 mL) vegan mayonnaise
6 tablespoons minced chives
2 teaspoons onion powder
1 teaspoon garlic powder
½ teaspoon salt
Black pepper, to taste
4 teaspoons apple cider vinegar
2 teaspoons maple syrup
4 cups (450 g) shaved cabbage
1 apple, julienned

Buffalo Sauce:

⅓ cup (80 mL) chili sauce, such as Heinz
2½ tablespoons maple syrup
1 tablespoon hot sauce, such as Frank's RedHot
1 tablespoon lime juice
½ teaspoon salt
½ teaspoon garlic powder
½ teaspoon vegan Worcestershire sauce

For the Apple Slaw:

1. In a large bowl, combine the soy cream, vegan mayonnaise, chives, onion powder, garlic powder, salt, pepper, vinegar, and maple syrup.

2. Add the cabbage and apple to the dressing. Toss to combine, then refrigerate for 1 hour before serving.

For the Buffalo Sauce:

3. In a small bowl, combine all the sauce ingredients. Set aside.

Recipe continues

Aïoli:

⅓ cup (80 mL) vegan mayonnaise
1 green onion, minced
1 teaspoon garlic powder
1½ teaspoons lime juice
1 teaspoon maple syrup
Salt and pepper, to taste

Tofu:

¼ cup (32 g) cornstarch
2 tablespoons nutritional yeast
1 teaspoon salt
1 pound (450 g) firm tofu, cut into sticks
3 tablespoons vegetable oil (approx.)

To Serve:

4 large tortillas
1 avocado, sliced
Cherry tomatoes, halved
Fresh cilantro leaves

For the Aïoli:

4. In another small bowl, combine all the aïoli ingredients. Set aside.

For the Tofu:

5. In a bowl, combine the cornstarch, yeast, and salt. Add the tofu sticks and gently toss to coat.

6. In a skillet over medium-high heat, heat the oil. Add the tofu sticks and fry for 10 minutes, flipping them halfway through and adding more oil if needed.

7. When the tofu sticks are golden brown, lower the heat and add the Buffalo sauce. Gently toss to coat the tofu with the sauce.

To Serve:

8. Spread some aïoli on each tortilla, then add some Buffalo tofu sticks, apple slaw, avocado slices, tomatoes, and cilantro. Roll up each tortilla to close, and serve with the remaining aïoli.

Tofegg Sandwiches

Serves 4 | Prep Time: 20 min | Cook Time: 10 min | Chill Time: 20 min

I love hiking, provided I'm rewarded with tofu sandwiches at the end of the trail. My wife teases me that as soon as we set foot on the trail, I start asking when we'll get to eat the sandwiches. The secret ingredient in these is the Himalayan black salt, which you can easily find online. It adds that hard-boiled-egg flavor to tofu. It's magic!

Tofu Eggs:

3 cups (750 mL) water
1½ teaspoons salt
2 tablespoons apple cider vinegar
1 lb (450 g) extra-firm tofu, coarsely crumbled

Mayonnaise:

¾ cup (180 mL) vegan mayonnaise
2 green onions, minced
1 stalk celery, diced
1 teaspoon garlic powder
¾ teaspoon Himalayan black salt
Pinch of ground turmeric (optional)
Black pepper, to taste
1 teaspoon maple syrup

To Serve:

8 slices of bread

For the Tofu Eggs:

1. In a large pot, bring the water to a boil. Add the salt, vinegar, and tofu, lower the heat, and simmer for 10 minutes.

2. Drain, transfer to a bowl, let cool completely, and refrigerate for 20 minutes.

For the Mayonnaise:

3. In a bowl, whisk together all the mayonnaise ingredients.

To Serve:

4. Add the tofu eggs to the mayonnaise and stir to combine.

5. Spread the tofu filling over a slice of bread, then close the sandwich with a second slice of bread. Repeat with remaining filling and bread.

Romesco Tofu with Garlic and Spinach Angel Hair Pasta

Serves 4 | Prep Time: 45 min | Cook Time: 40 min

Romesco is a rustic Catalonian sauce made with nuts and red bell peppers. In Spain, it is often served with grilled whole green onions, but it's wonderful with any grilled vegetables. Smoked paprika, roasted bell peppers, and cayenne pepper add plenty of personality to the sauce, as well as a slightly spicy edge. This dish is served over garlic and spinach angel hair pasta. Simply irresistible!

Romesco Sauce:

½ cup (57 g) slivered almonds

3 tablespoons olive oil, divided

1 cup (110 g) grated carrots

6 sun-dried tomatoes, minced

2 cloves garlic, minced

1 shallot, minced

1 jar (12 oz/340 mL) roasted red bell peppers, drained, rinsed, and finely chopped

1½ cups (375 mL) water

¼ cup (60 mL) soy cream

2 tablespoons nutritional yeast

1 teaspoon dried oregano

¾ teaspoon salt

¼ teaspoon smoked paprika

¼ teaspoon cayenne pepper

Black pepper, to taste

1 tablespoon tomato paste

1 tablespoon maple syrup

1 tablespoon lemon juice

For the Romesco Sauce:

1. In a skillet over medium heat, toast the almonds for about 2 minutes, stirring constantly, until lightly browned and fragrant. Transfer to a plate and set aside.

2. In the same skillet over medium heat, heat 2 tablespoons of the oil, then add the carrots, sun-dried tomatoes, garlic, shallot, and roasted peppers, and cook for 8 minutes, stirring frequently.

3. Stir in the toasted almonds and the remaining sauce ingredients, including the remaining oil. Bring to a boil, then remove from the heat.

4. Transfer the mixture to a blender and blend until smooth. Set aside.

Recipe continues

Tofu:

1 lb (450 g) firm tofu
¼ cup (32 g) cornstarch
2 tablespoons nutritional yeast
1 teaspoon salt
1 teaspoon garlic powder
½ teaspoon black pepper
3 tablespoons vegetable oil

Angel Hair Pasta:

10½ ounces (300 g) dried angel
    hair or spaghettini pasta
¼ cup (60 mL) olive oil
4 cloves garlic, minced
8 cups (140 g) baby spinach
¼ cup (15 g) nutritional yeast
¼ cup (60 mL) water
¾ teaspoon salt
½ teaspoon red pepper flakes

For the Tofu:

5. Cut the tofu widthwise into 12 equal slices, then cut each slice into 2 triangles.

6. In a bowl, combine the cornstarch, yeast, salt, garlic powder, and pepper. Add the tofu and toss to coat.

7. Wipe out the skillet used for the romesco sauce, add the oil and heat over medium-high heat, then add some of tofu triangles to cover the bottom of the skillet in a single layer. Fry the tofu for 10 minutes, flipping it halfway through. Transfer to a plate and set aside. Repeat to fry all the tofu.

For the Angel Hair Pasta:

8. Meanwhile, cook the pasta according to the package directions. Drain and set aside.

9. In a pot over medium heat, heat the oil, then add the garlic and cook, stirring, for 2 minutes, until light golden. Stir in the spinach, yeast, water, salt, and red pepper flakes, and cook, stirring, for 4 minutes. Add the cooked pasta and toss to reheat.

10. Divide the pasta among serving plates. Top with a few slices of tofu and drizzle with romesco sauce.

Tofish Burgers
with Tartar Sauce

Serves 4 | Prep Time: 40 min | Cook Time: 45 min | Rest Time: 15 min

The one thing I've been missing as a vegan is fish, but I found a trick to satisfy my cravings: adding nori to my recipes! Nori is a seaweed with a salty, oceanic taste similar to fish. Isn't that so handy? To create the texture of fish, I substitute hearts of palm. Chopped up, you'd swear they're crab or fish. The tartar sauce here deserves an honorable mention. It's so easy to prepare, yet so delicious, and it makes a great dip for fries or crudités.

Tofish Patties:

- 3 tablespoons olive oil
- 1 onion, minced
- 1 can (14 oz/398 mL) hearts of palm, rinsed, drained, and coarsely chopped
- 8 oz (225 g) firm tofu, finely chopped
- 2 sheets nori, coarsely chopped
- 2 cloves garlic, minced
- ⅓ cup (80 mL) white wine
- ½ cup (65 g) vital wheat gluten flour
- ¼ cup (25 g) quick-cooking oats
- 3 tablespoons breadcrumbs
- 3 tablespoons nutritional yeast
- 2 tablespoons maple syrup
- 1 teaspoon lemon juice
- 1 teaspoon onion powder
- ½ teaspoon salt
- ½ teaspoon celery salt
- ½ teaspoon mustard powder
- 3 tablespoons vegetable oil

For the Tofish Patties:

1. Preheat the oven to 375°F (190°C). Grease a baking sheet with oil.

2. In a skillet over medium heat, heat the olive oil, then add the onion and cook, stirring, for 5 minutes. Add the hearts of palm, tofu, nori, and garlic, and cook for 5 minutes, stirring from time to time. Stir in the wine and simmer until most of the liquid is absorbed.

3. Remove from the heat and stir in the remaining patty ingredients, except the vegetable oil.

4. Transfer the mixture to a food processor and pulse for 30 seconds, until the mixture can be shaped (it shouldn't be too smooth).

5. Shape the mixture into four 4- or 5-inch (10 or 13 cm) patties. At this stage, you can cook them right away, refrigerate them in an airtight container for up to 3 days, or freeze them for up to 3 months. To freeze, just set them on a lined baking sheet, 1 inch (2.5 cm) apart, and freeze for 1 hour before placing in an airtight container.

6. When ready to cook, transfer the patties to the prepared baking sheet, then brush each patty with vegetable oil. Bake for 25 to 30 minutes, or until the patties are lightly browned.

7. Turn off the oven and let the patties rest in the warm oven for 15 minutes before serving. (The patties will firm up as they cool.)

Recipe continues

Tartar Sauce:

½ cup (125 mL) vegan mayonnaise
3 tablespoons sweet relish
½ teaspoon garlic powder
¼ teaspoon salt
Black pepper, to taste
1 teaspoon maple syrup

To Serve:

4 hamburger buns
4 tomato slices
4 lettuce leaves

For the Tartar Sauce:

8. In a bowl, whisk together all the tartar sauce ingredients. Set aside.

To Serve:

9. Split the hamburger buns, place on an aluminum plate, and place in the oven with the patties for a few minutes, until warmed.

10. To assemble, fill each bun with a patty, spread with tartar sauce, and add a slice of tomato and a leaf of lettuce.

Tofish & Chips

Serves 4 | Prep Time: 40 min | Cook Time: 30 min

I spent a few weeks in England when I was younger and was very impressed with the fish and chips I sampled, so crispy and delicious! For my Tofish & Chips, I marinate the tofu in lemon juice and celery salt to add more flavor. Once breaded, the tofu truly has that classic fish and chips flavor! Served with tartar sauce, it's simply divine.

Tofish:

- 1 lb (450 g) extra-firm tofu
- 2 teaspoons lemon juice
- ½ teaspoon celery salt
- 1 sheet nori, minced
- 1 cup + 2 tablespoons (140 g) all-purpose flour
- 1 cup (250 mL) unsweetened soy milk
- 1 tablespoon nutritional yeast
- 1½ teaspoons salt
- 1 teaspoon baking soda
- 1 teaspoon onion powder
- 1 teaspoon apple cider vinegar
- Black pepper, to taste
- 1 tablespoon maple syrup
- Vegetable oil, for frying

Oven-Baked Fries:

- 2½ pounds (1 kg) yellow-fleshed potatoes
- ¼ cup (60 mL) vegetable oil
- 1 tablespoon steak spice mix

For the Tofish:

1. Cut the tofu widthwise into 8 equal slices. Place in a bowl and add the lemon juice and celery salt. Marinate for 20 minutes.

2. Meanwhile, in a large bowl, combine the remaining ingredients, except the oil, whisking until smooth. Set aside.

For the Oven-Baked Fries:

3. While the tofu is marinating, preheat the oven to 400°F (200°C).

4. Slice the potatoes into sticks (do not peel the potatoes). Transfer the potato sticks to a bowl, add the oil and steak spice mix, and toss to coat the sticks with the seasonings. Transfer to a baking sheet and spread out in a single layer.

5. Bake for 25 to 30 minutes, or until the fries are golden brown.

To Fry the Tofish:

6. Meanwhile, in a large pot or deep fryer, preheat 2½ inches (6 cm) vegetable oil to 350°F (180°C). Line a baking sheet with paper towels.

7. Dip each slice of tofu in the batter, then drop into the hot oil, 2 pieces at a time, and fry for 3 minutes, or until golden brown. Transfer the fried tofu to the prepared baking sheet to drain.

8. When all of the tofu is fried, divide it among serving plates and serve with fries.

Onion Tofu with Mashed Potatoes

Serves 4 | Prep Time: 45 min | Cook Time: 45 min

The secret is in the sauce! Tofu is rather neutral on its own, so it's essential to know how to season it properly. Many people marinate tofu to make it more flavorful, but I prefer serving it in a richly flavored sauce, to ensure all the flavor makes it to the plate. In this dish, tofu is tossed with a comforting onion sauce and served with seasoned mashed potatoes. The ultimate comfort food!

Tofu:

1 lb (450 g) firm tofu
Salt and black pepper, to taste
3 tablespoons vegetable oil

Mashed Potatoes:

2½ lbs (1 kg) yellow-fleshed potatoes, peeled and diced
¼ cup (15 g) nutritional yeast
¼ cup (60 mL) vegan butter
¼ cup (60 mL) soy cream
2 teaspoons salt
1 teaspoon onion powder

Onion Sauce:

3 tablespoons olive oil
2 onions, minced
½ cup (125 mL) white wine
2 tablespoons all-purpose flour
2 cups (500 mL) vegetable broth
¼ cup (15 g) nutritional yeast
2 tablespoons miso paste
2 tablespoons maple syrup
2 tablespoons tomato paste
1 tablespoon vegan Worcestershire sauce
1 tablespoon balsamic vinegar
¼ teaspoon red pepper flakes
Black pepper, to taste

For the Tofu:

1. Press the tofu using a tofu press, or wrap it in paper towels, sandwich between two baking sheets, set a heavy object on top, and let drain for 30 minutes.

2. Cut the tofu widthwise into 10 equal slices. Season with salt and pepper.

3. In a skillet over medium heat, heat the oil, then add the tofu slices and fry for 6 minutes, flipping them halfway through. Transfer to a plate and set aside.

For the Mashed Potatoes:

4. Place the potatoes in a large pot, cover with cold water, and bring to a boil. Lower the heat and simmer for 30 minutes, or until tender. Drain and transfer to a bowl.

5. Add the remaining mashed potato ingredients and use a potato masher to mash to a smooth consistency.

For the Onion Sauce:

6. Meanwhile, in the skillet you used to fry the tofu, heat the oil over medium-high heat, then add the onions and cook, stirring, for 10 minutes. Add the wine, bring to a boil, and cook until the liquid is fully evaporated, about 2 minutes.

7. Add the flour, stir to combine, then whisk in the broth. Stir in the remaining ingredients and bring to a boil, then lower the heat and simmer for 5 minutes. Return the tofu to the skillet and simmer to reheat.

8. Serve the fried tofu with the mashed potatoes.

Maple Leek and Mushroom Tofu

Serves 4 | Prep Time: 40 min | Cook Time: 30 min

Mushrooms are definitely one of my favorite vegetables, even though I know they're technically fungi, not vegetables. I love everything about mushrooms: their texture (when cooked properly), their umami-filled flavor, and their versatility. Mushrooms can even be substituted for meat in many recipes. In this recipe, my beloved mushrooms are combined with lightly breaded tofu and a white wine cream sauce. Believe me, there won't be leftovers!

Baked Baby Potatoes:

3 tablespoons olive oil

1 tablespoon nutritional yeast

½ teaspoon salt

½ teaspoon dried parsley or oregano

¼ teaspoon sweet paprika

Black pepper, to taste

1½ lbs (700 g) baby potatoes, halved

Crispy Tofu:

¼ cup (32 g) cornstarch

1 teaspoon salt

1 lb (450 g) firm tofu, diced

3 tablespoons vegetable oil

For the Baked Baby Potatoes:

1. Preheat the oven to 400°F (200°C).

2. In a large bowl, combine the oil, yeast, salt, parsley, paprika, and pepper. Add the potatoes and toss to coat. Transfer to a baking sheet and spread out in a single layer.

3. Bake for 25 to 30 minutes, or until the potatoes are golden brown.

For the Crispy Tofu:

4. Meanwhile, in a medium bowl, combine the cornstarch and salt. Add the tofu and gently toss to coat.

5. In a skillet over medium-high heat, heat the oil, then add the tofu and fry for 10 minutes, stirring from time to time. Transfer to a plate and set aside.

Recipe continues

White Wine Cream Sauce:

2 tablespoons olive oil

8 ounces (225 g) white button
   mushrooms, quartered

1½ cups (120 g) minced leeks

3 cloves garlic, minced

½ cup (65 g) frozen green peas

½ cup (125 mL) white wine

1 cup (250 mL) vegetable broth

2 tablespoons nutritional yeast

1 teaspoon salt

½ teaspoon mustard powder

½ teaspoon sweet paprika

½ teaspoon dried herbes de
   Provence

Black pepper, to taste

3 tablespoons maple syrup

1 tablespoon raspberry vinegar

2 teaspoons cornstarch mixed with
   2 tablespoons water

For the White Wine Cream Sauce:

6. In the same skillet over medium heat, heat the oil, then add the mushrooms and leeks, and cook, stirring, for 7 minutes. Stir in the garlic, peas, and wine. Increase the heat and bring to a boil, then lower the heat to medium and cook for 2 minutes.

7. Stir in the remaining ingredients, except the cornstarch mixture, and bring to a boil.

8. Stir in the fried tofu and the cornstarch mixture, and bring back to a boil, stirring constantly. Lower the heat and simmer for 2 minutes to thicken the sauce.

9. Serve the tofu and sauce with the baked baby potatoes.

Tofu with Creamy Mushroom Sauce and Kale Orzo

Serves 4 | **Prep Time: 45 min** | **Cook Time: 25 min**

Even if you think you don't like tofu, I guarantee that you're going to love this recipe. Most people who don't care for tofu complain about its texture, which can sometimes be mushy. Not my tofu! I coat it in cornstarch and fry it in oil to give it texture. Served in a creamy sauce over orzo and kale, this dish is a winner.

Tofu:

1 lb (450 g) firm tofu
¼ cup (32 g) cornstarch
1 tablespoon nutritional yeast
1 teaspoon salt
1 teaspoon garlic powder
½ teaspoon paprika
¼ cup (60 mL) vegetable oil

Cream Sauce:

¼ cup (60 mL) olive oil
2 portobello mushrooms, minced
1 onion, minced
3 cloves garlic, minced
3 tablespoons cognac
1 cup (250 mL) vegetable broth
½ cup (125 mL) soy cream
3 tablespoons nutritional yeast
1 teaspoon salt
¼ teaspoon ground chipotle pepper
¼ teaspoon dried thyme
Black pepper, to taste
3 tablespoons maple syrup
2 tablespoons miso paste
1 tablespoon whole-grain mustard
1 tablespoon vegan Worcestershire sauce

For the Tofu:

1. Cut the tofu widthwise into 8 equal slices, then cut each slice into 4 triangles.

2. In a bowl, combine the cornstarch, yeast, salt, garlic powder, and paprika. Add the tofu and toss to coat.

3. In a skillet over medium-high heat, heat the oil, then add the tofu and fry until crunchy, about 10 minutes, flipping it halfway through. Transfer to a plate and set aside.

For the Cream Sauce:

4. In the same skillet over medium heat, heat the oil, then add the mushrooms and onion, and cook, stirring, for 8 minutes. Add the garlic and cognac, and cook, stirring, for 1 minute.

5. Stir in the remaining sauce ingredients and bring to a boil, then lower the heat and simmer for 5 minutes. Add the fried tofu and toss to combine.

Recipe continues

Kale Orzo:

9 ounces (250 g) dried orzo pasta

2 kale leaves, stems discarded,
 leaves coarsely chopped

¼ cup (15 g) nutritional yeast

¼ cup (60 mL) soy cream

2 tablespoons minced chives

2 tablespoons olive oil

1 tablespoon maple syrup

1 tablespoon lemon juice

1 tablespoon water

1 teaspoon garlic powder

¾ teaspoon salt

½ teaspoon onion powder

Black pepper, to taste

For the Kale Orzo:

6. Meanwhile, in a large pot of boiling water, boil the orzo and kale for 12 minutes. Drain and transfer to a bowl.

7. Add the remaining orzo ingredients and stir to combine. Serve with the tofu.

"Bacon" and Sun-Dried Tomato Spaghetti

Serves 2 | Prep Time: 30 min | Cook Time: 30 min

One of the best ways to make people fall in love with tofu is to make them believe it's bacon! The keys to achieving this culinary sleight of hand are liquid smoke and maple syrup. Together, they give tofu a delicious maple-smoked bacon flavor.

Tofu Bacon:

8 oz (225 g) extra-firm tofu, finely crumbled

2 tablespoons cornstarch

3 tablespoons vegetable oil

¼ cup (60 mL) water

1 tablespoon nutritional yeast

½ teaspoon garlic powder

½ teaspoon onion powder

½ teaspoon salt

2 tablespoons maple syrup

2 tablespoons soy sauce

½ teaspoon liquid smoke

½ teaspoon hot sauce, such as Frank's RedHot

Spaghetti:

10½ ounces (300 g) dried spaghetti pasta

6 tablespoons (90 mL) olive oil, divided

2 portobello mushrooms, diced

2 shallots, minced

1 teaspoon salt

⅓ cup (80 mL) white wine

2 cups (300 g) cherry tomatoes, halved

1½ cups (90 g) fresh basil leaves, minced

6 sun-dried tomatoes, minced

4 cloves garlic, minced

¼ cup (15 g) nutritional yeast

1 tablespoon maple syrup

¼ teaspoon red pepper flakes

For the Tofu Bacon:

1. In a bowl, toss the crumbled tofu with the cornstarch

2. In a skillet over medium-high heat, heat the oil, then add the tofu and cook, stirring, for 8 to 10 minutes, until golden brown and crunchy.

3. Meanwhile, in a bowl, combine the remaining tofu bacon ingredients.

4. When the tofu is crunchy, add the combined ingredients, lower the heat, and simmer, stirring frequently, until the liquid is fully absorbed, about 4 minutes. Transfer the tofu bacon to a plate and set aside.

For the Spaghetti:

5. Cook the pasta according to the package directions. Drain and set aside.

6. Meanwhile, in the same skillet over medium-high heat, heat 3 tablespoons of the oil, then add the mushrooms, shallots, and salt, and cook, stirring frequently, until the vegetables are tender, about 8 minutes. Deglaze with the wine and cook, stirring, for 1 minute.

7. Add the cherry tomatoes, basil, sun-dried tomatoes, and garlic and cook for 4 minutes, stirring frequently. Add the yeast, maple syrup, and red pepper flakes, and cook, stirring, for 1 minute.

8. Add the cooked spaghetti and the remaining oil, and toss to reheat.

9. Divide the spaghetti between bowls and sprinkle with the tofu bacon.

Shawarma Tofu Wraps

Serves 4 | Prep Time: 30 min | Chill Time: 1 hour | Cook Time: 50 min

Shawarma is derived from the Turkish word for "turning," referring to the rotisserie cooking method. Shawarma typically features meat, but that's never stopped me before. I've adapted it to create a vegan version here, to my utmost satisfaction—and yours too, I'm sure. Served with oven-roasted potatoes, it's even better!

Shawarma Tofu:

1 lb (450 g) extra-firm tofu
3 cloves garlic, minced
2 tablespoons nutritional yeast
2 teaspoons sweet paprika
1 teaspoon mustard powder
1 teaspoon ground cumin
1 teaspoon salt
½ teaspoon smoked paprika
¼ teaspoon cayenne pepper
3 tablespoons water
2½ tablespoons olive oil
1½ tablespoons lemon juice
1½ tablespoons maple syrup

Oven-Roasted Potatoes:

¼ cup (60 mL) olive oil
1 tablespoon steak spice mix
4 to 5 yellow-fleshed potatoes (about 1¾ lbs/790 g), thinly sliced

To Serve:

Naan (page 51)
¼ red onion, minced
1 tomato, sliced
Handful of lettuce, chopped
½ English cucumber, sliced
Aïoli (page 124)

For the Shawarma Tofu:

1. Cut the tofu widthwise into 12 equal slices, then cut each slice into 2 triangles.

2. In an airtight container, combine all the remaining tofu ingredients. Add the tofu slices and toss to coat with the marinade. Cover and refrigerate for at least 1 hour or up to 24 hours.

3. Preheat the oven to 400°F (200°C). Grease a baking sheet with oil.

4. Set the marinated tofu slices on the prepared baking sheet. Brush with some of the marinade from the container, then discard the remaining marinade.

5. Bake for 20 minutes. Remove from the oven, leaving the oven on.

For the Oven-Roasted Potatoes:

6. In a bowl, combine the olive oil with the steak spice. Add the potatoes and toss to coat. Transfer to a baking sheet and spread out in a single layer.

7. Bake for 25 to 30 minutes, or until the potatoes are golden brown.

To Serve:

8. Place the shawarma tofu on naan breads and garnish with red onion, tomato, lettuce, cucumber, and aïoli. Serve with the oven-roasted potatoes.

Ratatouille Lasagna with Almond Ricotta

Serves 6 to 8 | **Prep Time: 50 min** | **Cook Time: 1 hour**

I wanted to name this dish "Ratalasagna," but my wife wouldn't let me. I don't understand why . . . Whatever its name, what's important is that this dish is a delicious combination of two of my all-time favorites: ratatouille and lasagna! The sauce is just spicy enough, and the almond ricotta is so delicious you'll want to eat it by the spoonful.

Almond Ricotta:

12 oz (350 g) firm tofu, coarsely chopped
1 cup (114 g) slivered almonds
6 tablespoons (22 g) minced chives
⅓ cup (80 mL) vegetable oil
¼ cup (15 g) nutritional yeast
2 teaspoons garlic powder
2 teaspoons onion powder
1½ teaspoons salt
2 tablespoons lemon juice
1 tablespoon apple cider vinegar
2 teaspoons maple syrup

Ratatouille Lasagna:

9 sheets dried lasagna pasta
Marinara Sauce (page 151)
2 to 3 zucchini, sliced into thin rounds
2 to 3 tomatoes, sliced into thin half-rounds
Olive oil, for brushing
Salt and black pepper, to taste

For the Almond Ricotta:

1. In a food processor, blend all the ricotta ingredients to a slightly grainy consistency. Set aside.

For the Ratatouille Lasagna:

2. Cook the pasta according to the package directions. Drain and set aside.

3. Preheat the oven to 375°F (190°C).

4. Pour one-quarter of the marinara sauce into a 9 × 13-inch (23 × 33 cm) baking dish and spread to cover the bottom of the dish. Set 3 lasagna noodles side by side over the sauce. Spread the almond ricotta in an even layer over the noodles. Top with another quarter of the sauce, then another layer of noodles, then another quarter of the sauce, then the remaining noodles, then the remaining sauce.

5. Fan out the zucchini and tomato slices over the lasagna, alternating between the two and covering the entire lasagna. Brush the vegetables with oil, then season with salt and pepper.

6. Bake for 50 minutes, or until the vegetables are lightly browned.

Stuffed Eggplant Rolls

Serves 12 | Prep Time: 1 hour | Cook Time: 80 min

This Italian-inspired dish is sure to become one of your favorite recipes. The filling, a combination of cashew ricotta, tofu, and spinach seasoned with sun-dried tomatoes and garlic, makes the dish! This savory filling is wrapped in tender eggplant slices, baked in a rich tomato sauce, and garnished with melted vegan cheese. What more could you want?

Marinara Sauce:

¼ cup (60 mL) olive oil
2 onions, minced
6 cloves garlic, minced
2 cans (each 28 oz/796 mL) diced
   tomatoes, with juice
⅓ cup (20 g) nutritional yeast
3 tablespoons cane sugar
1 tablespoon dried oregano
2 teaspoons dried basil
1½ teaspoons salt
½ teaspoon red pepper flakes
½ teaspoon mustard powder
3 bay leaves
Black pepper, to taste

Eggplant Rolls:

2 eggplants
¼ cup + 2 tablespoons (90 mL)
   olive oil, divided
2 teaspoons salt, divided
½ teaspoon black pepper
1 cup (140 g) cashews

For the Marinara Sauce:

1. In a pot over medium heat, heat the oil, then add the onions and cook, stirring, for 8 minutes, until tender. Add the garlic and cook for 2 minutes, stirring frequently.

2. Add the remaining sauce ingredients and bring to a boil, then lower the heat and simmer for 30 minutes, stirring from time to time. Discard the bay leaves. The sauce can be stored in an airtight container in the fridge for up to 4 days, or in the freezer for up to 3 months.

For the Eggplant Rolls:

3. Meanwhile, preheat the oven to 400°F (200°C). Grease a baking sheet with oil.

4. Cut each eggplant lengthwise into 5 equal slices about ½ inch (1 cm) thick, discarding the stem. Set the eggplant slices on the prepared baking sheet. Brush each slice with oil, using ¼ cup (60 mL) total, then season with 1 teaspoon of the salt and the pepper.

5. Bake for 30 minutes. Remove from the oven and set aside.

6. Meanwhile, soak the cashews in boiling water for 15 minutes. Drain and set aside.

Recipe continues

4 cloves garlic, minced

1 onion, minced

8 cups (140 g) baby spinach

6 sun-dried tomatoes

10½ oz (300 g) firm tofu, coarsely chopped

2 tablespoons nutritional yeast

1 tablespoon maple syrup

½ teaspoon red pepper flakes

2½ cups (225 g) grated vegan cheese

7. In a skillet, heat 2 tablespoons of oil over medium heat, then add the garlic, onion, and spinach, and cook, stirring, for 10 minutes.

8. Transfer the spinach mixture to a food processor, then add the cashews, sun-dried tomatoes, tofu, yeast, maple syrup, red pepper flakes, and the remaining salt. Blend until smooth. Let cool for 10 minutes.

9. Set the eggplant slices flat on a work surface. Spoon ¼ cup (65 g) of the filling along one end of each slice, then roll to enclose the filling. If needed, use a toothpick to secure the rolls, but don't forget to remove them before serving!

10. Pour 3 cups (750 mL) of the marinara sauce into a 9 × 13-inch (23 × 33 cm) baking dish and spread to cover the bottom of the dish. Set the eggplant rolls, seam side down, side by side over the sauce. Cover with the remaining sauce. Sprinkle with the vegan cheese.

11. Bake for 30 minutes, or until the cheese is melted and starting to brown.

Tandoori Tofu

Serves 4 | **Prep Time: 35 min** | **Chill Time: 1 hour** | **Cook Time: 20 min**

I love Indian cuisine, and I'm always trying to bring those flavors into my own cooking. What's great, as a vegan, is that many people in India do not eat meat, which means finding vegan options in Indian restaurants is always easy. But why not cook Indian food at home? It's easy and affordable, and the taste is simply extraordinary. In this recipe, tofu is infused with tangy spices, then served with a raita that adds creaminess and freshness to the dish. You can easily serve the raita as a dressing or a dip too!

Tandoori Tofu:

1 lb (450 g) firm tofu
¼ cup (60 mL) olive oil
2 tablespoons nutritional yeast
1 teaspoon ground ginger
1 teaspoon ground cumin
1 teaspoon onion powder
1 teaspoon garlic powder
1 teaspoon sweet paprika
1 teaspoon salt
¼ teaspoon cayenne pepper
Black pepper, to taste
2 tablespoons water
1 teaspoon maple syrup
1 teaspoon liquid smoke

Cumin Rice:

2 cups (500 mL) vegetable broth
1 cup (180 g) jasmine rice, rinsed
1 tablespoon olive oil
½ teaspoon cumin seeds
Pinch of saffron threads
Salt and black pepper, to taste
1 cup (130 g) frozen green peas

For the Tandoori Tofu:

1. Cut the tofu widthwise into 10 equal slices, then cut each slice into 2 triangles.

2. In an airtight container, combine the remaining tofu ingredients. Add the tofu, toss to coat with the marinade, cover, and refrigerate for at least 1 hour or up to 24 hours.

3. Preheat the oven to 400°F (200°C). Grease a baking sheet with oil.

4. Spread the tofu over the prepared baking sheet. Bake for 20 minutes, or until lightly browned.

For the Cumin Rice:

5. Meanwhile, in a saucepan, combine all the rice ingredients, except the peas. Bring to a boil, then lower the heat, cover, and simmer for 10 minutes, or until the liquid is fully absorbed.

6. Remove from the heat and add the peas. Let rest, covered, for 15 minutes. Stir before serving.

Recipe continues

Raita:

⅓ **English cucumber, finely diced**
½ **cup (125 mL) soy cream**
⅓ **cup (80 mL) vegan mayonnaise**
5 fresh mint leaves, minced
1 teaspoon onion powder
½ **teaspoon salt**
½ **teaspoon garlic powder**
Black pepper, to taste
1 tablespoon lime juice
1 teaspoon maple syrup

To Serve:

Red onion, minced
Cherry tomatoes, halved
Naan (page 51)

For the Raita:

7. In a bowl, combine all the raita ingredients.

To Serve:

8. Divide the rice among serving bowls, then add the tandoori tofu and garnish with red onion, cherry tomatoes, and raita. Serve with naan.

Lemongrass Tofu with Coconut Rice

Serves 4 | Prep Time: 50 min | Cook Time: 25 min

Lemongrass tofu is one of my favorite ways to serve tofu. It's so quick and easy to prepare, and simply delicious, especially when served with coconut rice. I learned to appreciate coconuts while traveling through Thailand. So many of the dishes I sampled featured amazing fragrance and texture, all due to the mighty coconut. I couldn't wait to start incorporating more coconut into my cooking.

Lemongrass Sauce:

2 stalks lemongrass
2 cups (500 mL) vegetable broth
¼ cup (55 g) packed brown sugar
1 sheet nori, torn into small pieces
3 tablespoons soy sauce
1 tablespoon rice vinegar
1 teaspoon sriracha
Black pepper, to taste

Coconut Rice:

1 tablespoon vegetable oil
1 shallot, minced
1 clove garlic, minced
1 cup (180 g) jasmine rice, rinsed
¾ cup (180 mL) coconut milk
¾ cup (180 mL) vegetable broth
½ teaspoon salt

For the Lemongrass Sauce:

1. To prepare the lemongrass, cut off both ends of each stalk, then peel off the two first leaves, which tend to be stiffer. Score the lemongrass stalks several times, then hit them with the back of a knife blade to bruise them.

2. In a bowl, combine the prepared lemongrass with the remaining sauce ingredients and let rest for at least 30 minutes, to allow the lemongrass to infuse the sauce.

For the Coconut Rice:

3. In a large pot over medium heat, heat the oil, then add the shallot and garlic, and cook, stirring, for 2 to 3 minutes, or until the garlic is lightly browned.

4. Stir in the remaining rice ingredients and bring to a boil, then lower the heat and simmer for 10 minutes, or until the liquid is fully absorbed.

5. Remove from the heat and let rest, covered, for at least 10 minutes. Stir before serving.

Recipe continues

Tofu:

¼ cup (32 g) cornstarch

2 tablespoons nutritional yeast

½ teaspoon garlic powder

½ teaspoon salt

1 lb (450 g) firm tofu, diced

¼ cup + 3 tablespoons (105 mL) vegetable oil, divided

¼ cup (14 g) dried sliced shiitake mushrooms, rehydrated and drained

2 shallots, minced

2 cloves garlic, minced

1 tablespoon minced fresh ginger

2 teaspoons cornstarch mixed with 2 tablespoons water

For the Tofu:

6. Meanwhile, in a bowl, combine the cornstarch, yeast, garlic powder, and salt. Add the tofu and gently toss to coat.

7. In a skillet over medium-high heat, heat ¼ cup (60 mL) oil, then add the tofu and fry for 10 minutes, stirring frequently. Transfer to a plate and set aside.

8. In the same skillet over medium-high heat, heat 3 tablespoons oil, then add the mushrooms, shallots, garlic, and ginger, and cook, stirring, for 5 minutes.

9. Stir in the lemongrass sauce and bring to a boil, then lower the heat and simmer for 5 minutes, stirring regularly.

10. Stir in the cornstarch mixture and bring back to a boil, then lower the heat and simmer for 1 minute, stirring constantly. Add the fried tofu and stir to combine. Discard the lemongrass.

11. Serve the tofu and sauce with the coconut rice.

Balsamic Tofu with Cauliflower and Corn Puree

Serves 4 | Prep Time: 15 min | Cook Time: 20 min

For this dish, I turn to many of my favorite flavor boosters to make it as delicious as possible. I use miso for depth and saltiness; nutritional yeast for a savory touch; balsamic vinegar for bittersweet notes; and maple syrup to perfectly balance the acidity of the vinegar. Don't you dare skip the cauliflower and corn puree: it's simply divine!

Roasted Asparagus:

1 pound (450 g) asparagus
1½ tablespoons nutritional yeast
¼ teaspoon garlic powder
¼ teaspoon salt
Black pepper, to taste
3 tablespoons olive oil

Cauliflower and Corn Puree:

1 medium cauliflower, cut into florets
2½ cups (410 g) frozen corn kernels
3 cloves garlic, peeled and smashed
2 tablespoons nutritional yeast
1½ teaspoons salt
1 teaspoon onion powder
Black pepper, to taste
2 tablespoons soy cream
2 tablespoons vegan butter
2 teaspoons lemon juice

For the Roasted Asparagus:

1. Preheat the oven to 375°F (190°C).

2. Slice off and discard the bottom third of each asparagus stalk.

3. In a large bowl, combine the yeast, garlic powder, salt, pepper, and oil. Add the asparagus and toss to coat. Transfer to a baking sheet and spread out in a single layer.

4. Roast for about 20 minutes, or until lightly browned on the edges.

For the Cauliflower and Corn Puree:

5. Meanwhile, in a large pot of boiling water, boil the cauliflower, corn, and garlic for 20 minutes, until the vegetables are tender. Drain and transfer to a bowl.

6. Add the remaining puree ingredients to the bowl and, using an immersion blender or a potato masher, puree to a smooth consistency.

Recipe continues

Balsamic Tofu:

¼ cup (32 g) cornstarch

1½ teaspoons salt, divided

1 pound (450 g) firm tofu, diced

3 tablespoons vegetable oil

1 tablespoon nutritional yeast

1 teaspoon garlic powder

½ teaspoon onion powder

Black pepper, to taste

3 tablespoons maple syrup

3 tablespoons water

2 tablespoons balsamic vinegar

1 tablespoon miso paste

2 teaspoons Dijon mustard

1 teaspoon hot sauce, such as Frank's RedHot

For the Balsamic Tofu:

7. While the vegetables are cooking, in a bowl, combine the cornstarch and 1 teaspoon salt. Add the tofu and gently toss to coat.

8. In a skillet over medium-high heat, heat the oil, then add the tofu and fry for 10 minutes, stirring frequently. Transfer to a plate.

9. In the same skillet, combine the remaining tofu ingredients, including the remaining salt. Return the fried tofu to the sauce and bring to a boil, then lower the heat and cook for 2 minutes, or until the liquid is almost fully absorbed. Remove from the heat.

10. Serve the tofu with the cauliflower and corn puree and the roasted asparagus.

Greek Tofu with Tzatziki and Vegetable Rice

Serves 4 | **Prep Time: 10 min** | **Chill Time: 1 hour** | **Cook Time: 20 min**

A couple of years ago I visited Greece and quickly realized vegan options were limited, especially on the islands. I promised myself that I would create a Greek-inspired vegan dish as soon as I got home—and I did just that. The tofu is marinated in a combination of mustard, red wine vinegar, and herbs, and then it's roasted in the oven until crisp. A flavorful cucumber-based tzatziki and a surprising vegetable rice complete this dish. Let your tastebuds travel while you stay at home!

Marinated Tofu:

1 lb (450 g) extra-firm tofu
2 tablespoons whole-grain mustard
2 tablespoons maple syrup
2 tablespoons olive oil
1 tablespoon red wine vinegar
1 teaspoon dried oregano
1 teaspoon dried basil
1 teaspoon salt
¼ teaspoon red pepper flakes
Black pepper, to taste

Vegetable Rice:

2 tablespoons olive oil
1 onion, minced
2 cups (500 mL) vegetable broth
1 cup (180 g) long-grain white rice, rinsed
1 teaspoon salt
Black pepper, to taste
½ cup (65 g) frozen green peas
½ cup (80 g) frozen corn kernels

To Serve:

Naan (page 51)
Tzatziki (page 40)
Cherry tomatoes, quartered

For the Marinated Tofu:

1. Tear the tofu into small bites.

2. In an airtight container, combine the remaining tofu ingredients. Add the tofu, toss to coat with the marinade, cover, and refrigerate for at least 1 hour or up to 24 hours.

3. Preheat the oven to 400°F (200°C). Grease a baking sheet with oil.

4. Spread the tofu over the prepared baking sheet. Bake for 20 minutes, or until lightly browned.

For the Vegetable Rice:

5. Meanwhile, in a pot over medium heat, heat the oil, then add the onion and cook, stirring, for 5 minutes. Stir in the broth, rice, salt, and pepper, and bring to a boil, then lower the heat, cover, and simmer for about 12 minutes, or until the liquid is fully absorbed.

6. Remove from the heat and add the peas and corn. Let rest, covered, for 15 minutes. Stir before serving.

To Serve:

7. Serve the marinated tofu with the vegetable rice, naan, tzatziki, and cherry tomatoes.

Orange Tofu

Serves 4 | Prep Time: 30 min | Cook Time: 20 min | Rest Time: 20 min

This dish is inspired by the classic Chinese takeout dish orange chicken. Infused with irresistible citrus and ginger flavors, and overflowing with veggies such as red bell pepper and green onions, this recipe is surprisingly easy to make. But don't forget the sriracha! It gives the dish an irresistible spicy kick.

Quinoa:

2 cups (500 mL) vegetable broth
1 cup (170 g) quinoa, rinsed
¼ teaspoon salt

Tofu:

¼ cup (32 g) cornstarch
1 teaspoon salt
1 lb (450 g) firm tofu, diced
3 tablespoons vegetable oil

Orange Sauce:

3 tablespoons vegetable oil
3 green onions, minced
1 red bell pepper, diced
3 cloves garlic, minced
1 tablespoon minced fresh ginger
1 cup (250 mL) orange juice
¼ cup (60 mL) maple syrup
2 tablespoons soy sauce
1 tablespoon rice vinegar
1 teaspoon sriracha
½ teaspoon salt
Black pepper, to taste
1 tablespoon cornstarch mixed with 2 tablespoons water

For the Quinoa:

1. Pour the broth into a saucepan, stir in the quinoa and salt, cover, and set over medium-high heat. Bring to a boil, then lower the heat and simmer for 20 minutes, or until the broth is fully absorbed.

2. Remove from the heat and let rest, covered, for 20 minutes, then use a fork to fluff up the quinoa. Set aside.

For the Tofu:

3. Meanwhile, in a bowl, combine the cornstarch and salt. Add the tofu and gently toss to coat.

4. In a skillet over medium-high heat, heat the oil, then add the tofu and fry for 10 minutes, stirring frequently. Transfer to a plate and set aside.

For the Orange Sauce:

5. In the same skillet, heat the oil over medium-high heat, then add the green onions and bell pepper, reduce the heat to medium, and cook for 5 minutes, stirring frequently. Add the garlic and ginger, and cook for 2 minutes.

6. Stir in the remaining sauce ingredients, except the cornstarch mixture. Bring to a boil, reduce the heat to medium and cook for 4 minutes.

7. Stir in the cornstarch mixture and bring back to a boil, stirring constantly. Add the fried tofu and toss to reheat.

8. Serve the tofu and sauce over the quinoa.

Sweet-and-Sour Tofu

Serves 4 | Prep Time: 30 min | Cook Time: 20 min

I love recipes that combine sweet, salty, acidic, and spicy flavors. When the perfect balance between these flavors is reached, you get a truly magical dish. But if even just one of those flavors overpowers the others—too sweet, too acidic, too salty, or too spicy—then the dish might disappoint. This recipe is the delicious result when all are perfectly balanced!

Basmati Rice:

1 cup (190 g) basmati rice, rinsed
1½ cups (375 mL) water
¼ teaspoon salt

Tofu:

¼ cup (32 g) cornstarch
1 teaspoon salt
1 lb (450 g) firm tofu, diced
3 tablespoons vegetable oil

Apricot Sauce:

3 tablespoons vegetable oil
1 orange bell pepper, sliced
3 cups (200 g) broccoli florets
3 green onions, minced
1 cup (250 mL) water
½ cup (125 mL) sweet apricot jam
2 tablespoons soy sauce
2 tablespoons ketchup
1 tablespoon rice vinegar
1 teaspoon mustard powder
1 teaspoon sriracha
½ teaspoon salt
Black pepper, to taste
**2 teaspoons cornstarch mixed with
    2 tablespoons water**

For the Basmati Rice:

1. In a large pot, combine the rice, water, and salt. Bring to a boil, then lower the heat, cover, and simmer until the liquid is fully absorbed, about 10 minutes.

2. Remove from the heat and let rest, covered, for 10 minutes.

For the Tofu:

3. Meanwhile, in a bowl, combine the cornstarch and salt. Add the tofu and gently toss to coat.

4. In a skillet over medium-high heat, heat the oil, then add the tofu and fry for 10 minutes, stirring frequently. Transfer to a plate and set aside.

For the Apricot Sauce:

5. In the same skillet over medium-high heat, heat the oil, then add the bell pepper and cook, stirring, for 3 minutes. Add the broccoli and green onions, and cook, stirring, for 3 minutes.

6. Stir in the remaining sauce ingredients, except the cornstarch mixture, and cook for 2 minutes.

7. Stir in the cornstarch mixture and bring to a boil, stirring constantly. Add the fried tofu and toss to reheat.

8. Serve the tofu and sauce with the basmati rice.

Desserts

Vegan Chocolate Chip Cookies

Makes 12 cookies | Prep Time: 15 min | Chill Time: 30 min | Cook Time: 30 min

There's no age limit for appreciating chocolate chip cookies—especially when they're freshly baked and enjoyed warm with a glass of milk . . . soy milk, obviously. This recipe makes for a fun and easy afternoon baking project, so put on your apron, gather up the kids, and make these wonderful cookies.

2¾ cups (340 g) all-purpose flour

1 teaspoon baking soda

1 teaspoon baking powder

½ teaspoon salt

1 cup (250 mL) vegan butter

½ cup (110 g) packed brown sugar

½ cup (100 g) granulated sugar

¼ cup (60 mL) unsweetened soy milk

1 teaspoon vanilla extract

1 cup (170 g) vegan chocolate chips

1. In a medium bowl, combine the flour, baking soda, baking powder, and salt.

2. In a large bowl, whisk together or use a hand mixer to beat the vegan butter, brown sugar, and granulated sugar, for 3 minutes. Add the soy milk and vanilla, and whisk or beat for 1 minute.

3. Add the flour mixture to the vegan butter mixture and stir to combine. Stir in the chocolate chips. Refrigerate for 30 minutes to let the dough rest.

4. Meanwhile, preheat the oven to 375°F (190°C). Line two baking sheets with parchment paper.

5. Using a 3-tablespoon (45 mL) ice-cream scoop, divide the dough into 12 balls. Set 6 balls on each prepared baking sheet, spacing them out to allow them to spread.

6. Bake, one sheet at a time, for 12 to 15 minutes, or until the cookies are light golden brown around the edges but still soft in the center. Let cool on the baking sheets. The cookies will keep in an airtight container at room temperature for up to 5 days.

Molasses Cookies

Makes 12 cookies | Prep Time: 20 min | Chill Time: 50 min | Cook Time: 15 min

These homemade molasses cookies will always remind me of my grandmother's recipe. As it was in her recipe, the secret of my molasses cookies is the spice mix of ginger, cinnamon, and cloves. The smell of these cookies baking is the smell of the holidays in my house. Served warm, they are absolutely fantastic.

1 cup (250 mL) vegan butter
1 cup (250 mL) fancy molasses
½ cup (110 g) packed brown sugar
1 teaspoon apple cider vinegar
3⅓ cups (415 g) all-purpose flour
1 teaspoon baking soda
1 teaspoon ground ginger
1 teaspoon salt
½ teaspoon ground cinnamon
½ teaspoon baking powder
Pinch ground cloves

1. In a saucepan over medium heat, warm the vegan butter and molasses, stirring until the butter is melted (do not boil). Transfer to a bowl, stir to combine, then refrigerate for 30 minutes.

2. Stir the brown sugar and vinegar into the vegan butter mixture.

3. In a large bowl, whisk together the flour, baking soda, ginger, salt, cinnamon, baking powder, and cloves. Add the vegan butter mixture and stir to combine. Refrigerate for 20 minutes.

4. Meanwhile, preheat the oven to 375°F (190°C). Line two baking sheets with parchment paper.

5. Using a 3-tablespoon (45 mL) ice-cream scoop, divide the dough into 12 balls. Set 6 balls on each prepared baking sheet, spacing them out to allow them to spread.

6. Bake for 12 to 15 minutes, rotating baking sheets halfway through, or until light golden. Transfer the cookies to a wire rack and let cool for a few minutes. The cookies will keep in an airtight container at room temperature for up to 5 days.

Almond Cookies

Makes 12 cookies | **Prep Time: 15 min** | **Chill Time: 30 min** | **Cook Time: 15 min**

These cookies are perfect: crunchy on the outside but tender on the inside. And they're easy to make, too. Rolling them in sugar before baking puts them over the top. It's a little trick I learned from my grandma, and it adds an irresistible sweet crunchiness to the cookies.

1½ cups (190 g) all-purpose flour

1 cup (96 g) almond flour

1 teaspoon salt

1 teaspoon baking powder

1½ cups (300 g) granulated sugar, divided

1 cup (250 mL) vegan butter

¼ cup (60 mL) unsweetened soy milk

1 teaspoon vanilla extract

1. Preheat the oven to 400°F (200°C). Line two baking sheets with parchment paper.

2. In a large bowl, whisk together the flours, salt, and baking powder.

3. In another bowl, whisk together or use a hand mixer to beat 1 cup of sugar and the vegan butter, for 2 minutes. Add the soy milk and vanilla, and whisk or beat for 1 minute.

4. Add the sugar mixture to the flour mixture and whisk or beat for 1 minute. Refrigerate the dough for 30 minutes.

5. Using a ¼-cup (60 mL) ice-cream scoop, divide the dough into 12 balls. Roll each ball in the remaining sugar, then place on the prepared baking sheets, spacing them out to allow them to spread.

6. Bake for about 13 minutes, rotating baking sheets halfway through, or until the edges of the cookies are light golden. Do not overbake. Transfer the cookies to a wire rack and let cool for a few minutes. The cookies will keep in an airtight container for up to 5 days.

Pets-de-sœur

Makes 12 rounds │ **Prep Time: 30 min** │ **Chill Time: 30 min** │ **Cook Time: 45 min**

Pets-de-sœur is a traditional French-Canadian holiday dessert, typical of Quebec and the Acadia region of the Maritimes. My mom would make it using the pastry scraps left over after making her batches of savory and sweet pies, but this recipe's so good it's worth making the dough just for it. If you've got a sweet tooth, you've got to give this dessert a try! I'll leave you to google what the name translates to in English . . .

Pie Dough:

3 cups (375 g) all-purpose flour
1 teaspoon salt
1 cup (250 mL) vegan butter, chilled
⅔ cup plus 1 teaspoon (165 mL) ice water

Pets-de-sœur:

2 tablespoons vegan butter
1½ cups (330 g) packed brown sugar, divided
1 cup (250 mL) water

For the Pie Dough:

1. In a large bowl, combine the flour and salt. Using a pastry cutter or two knives, incorporate the vegan butter into the flour until the mixture is crumbly, with pea-sized chunks. Stir in the ice water.

2. Bring the pastry together into a ball, being careful not to overwork it. Cover with plastic wrap and refrigerate for at least 30 minutes and no longer than 1 hour.

For the Pets-de-sœur:

3. Preheat the oven to 375°F (190°C).

4. On a floured work surface, roll out the dough into a 12-inch (30 cm) square. Brush with the vegan butter, then evenly sprinkle with ¼ cup (60 mL) of the brown sugar. Roll up the dough to enclose the filling. Slice the roll into 12 rounds.

5. Set the rounds in an 8 × 11-inch (20 × 28 cm) rectangular or 10-inch (25 cm) round baking dish. Pour the water over the dough and sprinkle with the remaining brown sugar.

6. Bake for 40 to 45 minutes, or until golden brown. Pets-de-sœur can be stored for 5 days in an airtight container in the fridge.

Flaky Apple Tart

Serves 6 | **Prep Time: 30 min** | **Cook Time: 30 min**

I'm not a dessert person, generally speaking, but I'm crazy for apple tart. Flaky pastry and soft apples . . . what's not to like? This is my favorite dessert.

5 sheets phyllo pastry

⅓ cup (80 mL) vegetable oil

5 apples, cored, peeled, and thinly sliced

⅓ cup (70 g) granulated sugar

1 teaspoon ground cinnamon

1. Preheat the oven to 350°F (180°C). Grease a baking sheet with oil.

2. Place 1 sheet of phyllo pastry on the prepared baking sheet. Lightly brush with oil all over. Top with a second sheet, brush with oil, and repeat until all the phyllo is layered and brushed.

3. Fan out the apple slices over the pastry, leaving a 2-inch (5 cm) border all around. Sprinkle the apples with sugar and cinnamon. Fold the pastry border in toward the apples and brush the border with oil.

4. Bake for 30 minutes, or until the pastry is golden and the apples are tender. Let cool for 10 minutes before serving.

Oreo Cheesecake

Serves 6 | **Prep Time: 20 min** | **Cook Time: 15 min** | **Chill Time: 1 hour**

Oreo cookies are one of those "I didn't know they were vegan" ingredients. Lucky for us, because that means we get to enjoy this decadent cheesecake. Cashews make such a wonderful substitute for cream cheese, you won't even notice it's missing. Simply irresistible!

Crust:

2½ cups (275 g) Oreo Baking Crumbs
¼ cup (60 mL) vegan butter, melted

Filling:

1½ cups (210 g) cashews
1 can (14 oz/398 mL) coconut milk
⅓ cup (80 mL) maple syrup
1 tablespoon cornstarch
1 tablespoon lemon juice
2 teaspoons powdered agar-agar
1 teaspoon vanilla extract
¼ teaspoon salt

5 Oreo cookies, crushed, for garnish

For the Crust:

1. Preheat the oven to 375°F (190°C).

2. In a bowl, combine the baking crumbs and vegan butter until the mixture begins to clump.

3. Transfer the mixture to an 8½-inch (22 cm) springform pan and firmly press it down over the bottom of the pan.

4. Bake for 10 minutes. Remove from the oven and set aside.

For the Filling:

5. Meanwhile, soak the cashews in boiling water for 15 minutes. Drain.

6. In a blender, combine the soaked cashews, coconut milk, maple syrup, cornstarch, lemon juice, agar-agar, vanilla, and salt. Blend until smooth.

7. Pour the mixture into a saucepan and bring to a boil, stirring constantly. Boil for 1 minute, then remove from the heat.

8. Pour the filling mixture over the crust. With a wet spoon, smooth out the top of the cake. Refrigerate for at least 1 hour or up to 5 hours before serving.

9. Before serving, unmold the cake and garnish with the crushed Oreo cookies. The cake will keep in an airtight container in the fridge for up to 4 days.

Chocolate Mug Cake

Serves 1 | Prep Time: 5 min | Cook Time: 1 min

Sometimes when a sweet craving hits, I don't have the time to bake a wedding cake—I need something sweet then and there! In those times of need, I use this recipe to make a soft, gooey cake in no time.

2 tablespoons all-purpose flour

2 tablespoons unsweetened cocoa powder

2 tablespoons granulated sugar

¼ teaspoon baking powder

Pinch of salt

3 tablespoons unsweetened soy milk

1 tablespoon vegetable oil

½ teaspoon vanilla extract

2 tablespoons vegan chocolate chips

1. In a mug, combine the flour, cocoa, sugar, baking powder, and salt. Stir in the soy milk, oil and vanilla. Sprinkle the chocolate chips on top.

2. Microwave on High for 40 seconds. At this stage, the cake will be runny in the center, which is my favorite. For a fully set cake, cook for 20 seconds longer.

Queen Elizabeth Cake

Serves 8 | **Prep Time: 40 min** | **Cook Time: 65 min** | **Rest Time: 20 min**

If there's one dessert that makes me nostalgic, it's Queen Elizabeth cake, a delightful cake topped with a scrumptious coconut icing that becomes sticky when broiled. When I was a kid, this was my mother's favorite dessert. She would bake one, then slice it into portions and freeze it, which meant we always had Queen Elizabeth cake on hand to satisfy our cravings. I especially remember how much I loved that caramelized coconut topping. Don't tell my mom, but I think my version of the cake is even better than hers!

Queen Elizabeth Cake:

2¼ cups (280 g) all-purpose flour
1 cup (96 g) almond flour
¾ cup (165 g) packed brown sugar
½ cup (100 g) granulated sugar
2 teaspoons baking powder
1 teaspoon baking soda
1 teaspoon salt
1 cup (250 mL) coconut milk
½ cup (125 mL) unsweetened
  applesauce
⅓ cup (80 mL) vegetable oil
2 teaspoons apple cider vinegar
2 teaspoons lemon juice
1 teaspoon vanilla extract

Frosting:

2 cups (100 g) sweetened shredded
  coconut
½ cup (125 mL) coconut milk
⅓ cup (73 g) packed brown sugar
2 teaspoons lemon juice
1 teaspoon vanilla extract
¼ teaspoon salt

For the Queen Elizabeth Cake:

1. Preheat the oven to 350°F (180°C). Line the bottom of a 9-inch (23 cm) springform pan with parchment paper and grease the sides with oil.

2. In a large bowl, whisk together the flours, sugars, baking powder, baking soda, and salt.

3. In another bowl, whisk together or use a hand mixer to beat together the coconut milk, applesauce, oil, vinegar, lemon juice, and vanilla.

4. Add the coconut milk mixture to the flour mixture and stir until smooth.

5. Transfer the batter to the prepared pan and smooth to an even layer.

6. Bake for 1 hour, or until a toothpick inserted in the center comes out clean. Remove the cake from the oven, but do not unmold. Set the oven to broil.

For the Frosting:

7. In a bowl, whisk together all the frosting ingredients. Spread the frosting over the top of the hot cake.

8. Broil for 2 to 3 minutes, or until the frosting is light golden. Watch closely to make sure it doesn't burn. Let cool for 20 minutes before unmolding. The cake will keep in an airtight container in the fridge for up to 5 days.

Pouding Chômeur

Serves 6 to 8 | **Prep Time: 35 min** | **Cook Time: 50 min**

I challenge you to find a dessert more decadent than this Quebecois maple pudding, which combines a cloud-like cake with a rich maple syrup. It's the perfect dessert!

Syrup:

1½ cups (330 g) packed brown sugar
2 cups (500 mL) water
1 cup (250 mL) maple syrup
2 tablespoons vegan butter

Cake:

2½ cups (310 g) all-purpose flour
1 teaspoon baking powder
1 teaspoon baking soda
½ teaspoon salt
1 cup (200 g) granulated sugar
½ cup (125 mL) vegan butter
1 cup (250 mL) unsweetened soy milk
1 teaspoon vanilla extract

For the Syrup:

1. In a saucepan, combine all the syrup ingredients and bring to a boil. Remove from the heat and set aside.

For the Cake:

2. Preheat the oven to 400°F (200°C).

3. In a large bowl, whisk together the flour, baking powder, baking soda, and salt. Set aside.

4. In another bowl, whisk together or use a hand mixer to beat the sugar and vegan butter for 2 minutes. Add the soy milk and vanilla, and whisk or beat for 1 minute.

5. Add the sugar mixture to the flour mixture and stir until smooth.

6. Transfer the batter to a 9 × 13-inch (23 × 33 cm) baking dish and spread into an even layer. Spoon the syrup over the batter.

7. Bake for 40 to 45 minutes, or until golden brown.

Trio of Vegan Cupcakes

I have to admit that my wife, Amélie, helped me create these cupcake recipes. She obviously has taste . . . just look who she married!

RAINBOW CUPCAKES Makes 12 cupcakes | Prep Time: 30 min | Cook Time: 20 min

Cupcakes:

2¼ cups (280 g) all-purpose flour

1 cup (96 g) almond flour

1 cup (200 g) granulated sugar

2 tablespoons rainbow cake sprinkles

2 teaspoons baking powder

1 teaspoon baking soda

1 teaspoon salt

1 cup (250 mL) unsweetened soy milk

⅓ cup + 2 tablespoons (110 mL) unsweetened applesauce

⅓ cup (80 mL) vegetable oil

2 tablespoons apple cider vinegar

1 teaspoon vanilla extract

Frosting:

3¼ cups (390 g) powdered sugar

3 tablespoons + 1 teaspoon unsweetened soy milk

3 tablespoons vegan butter

1 teaspoon lime juice

1 teaspoon vanilla extract

Pinch of salt

2 tablespoons rainbow cake sprinkles

For the Cupcakes:

1. Preheat the oven to 375°F (190°C). Line a 12-cup muffin pan with paper cups or grease the cups generously with oil.

2. In a large bowl, whisk together the flours, sugar, sprinkles, baking powder, baking soda, and salt. Set aside.

3. In another bowl, whisk together the soy milk, applesauce, oil, vinegar, and vanilla.

4. Add the soy milk mixture to the flour mixture and stir to combine.

5. Using a ⅓-cup (80 mL) ice-cream scoop, divide the batter among the prepared muffin cups.

6. Bake for 20 minutes, or until a toothpick inserted in the center of a cupcake comes out clean. Remove the cupcakes from the pan, transfer to a wire rack, and let cool completely before frosting. Store in an airtight container in the fridge for up to 5 days.

For the Frosting:

7. In a bowl, whisk together or use a hand mixer to beat together all the frosting ingredients, except the sprinkles.

8. Frost the cupcakes using a knife or a pastry bag fitted with a round or fluted tip. Sprinkle the frosting with rainbow sprinkles.

MOCHA CUPCAKES   Makes 12 cupcakes | Prep Time: 30 min | Cook Time: 20 min

Cupcakes:

2¼ cups (280 g) all-purpose flour

1 cup (96 g) almond flour

1 cup (200 g) granulated sugar

3 tablespoons unsweetened cocoa powder

2 teaspoons baking powder

1 teaspoon baking soda

1 teaspoon salt

3 tablespoons instant coffee granules

1 cup (250 mL) unsweetened soy milk, at room temperature

⅓ cup + 2 tablespoons (110 mL) unsweetened applesauce

⅓ cup (80 mL) vegetable oil

2 tablespoons apple cider vinegar

1 teaspoon vanilla extract

Frosting:

3¼ cups (390 g) powdered sugar

1 tablespoon unsweetened cocoa powder

3 tablespoons + 2 teaspoons unsweetened soy milk, at room temperature

3 tablespoons vegan butter

2 teaspoons instant coffee granules

1 teaspoon lemon juice

1 teaspoon vanilla extract

Pinch of salt

For the Cupcakes:

1. Preheat the oven to 375°F (190°C). Line a 12-cup muffin pan with paper cups or grease the cups generously with oil.

2. In a large bowl, whisk together the flours, sugar, cocoa, baking powder, baking soda, and salt. Set aside.

3. In another bowl, dissolve the instant coffee in the soy milk. Whisk in the applesauce, oil, vinegar, and vanilla.

4. Add the coffee mixture to the flour mixture and stir to combine.

5. Using a ⅓-cup (80 mL) ice-cream scoop, divide the batter among the prepared muffin cups.

6. Bake for 20 minutes, or until a toothpick inserted in the center of a cupcake comes out clean. Remove the cupcakes from the pan, transfer to a wire rack, and let cool completely before frosting.

For the Frosting:

7. In a bowl, whisk together or use a hand mixer to beat together all the frosting ingredients.

8. Frost the cupcakes using a knife or a pastry bag fitted with a round or fluted tip.

RED VELVET CUPCAKES Makes 12 cupcakes | Prep Time: 30 min | Cook Time: 20 min

Cupcakes:

2¼ cups (280 g) all-purpose flour

1 cup (96 g) almond flour

1 cup (200 g) granulated sugar

1½ tablespoons unsweetened cocoa powder

2 teaspoons baking powder

1 teaspoon baking soda

1 teaspoon salt

1 cup (250 mL) unsweetened soy milk

⅓ cup + 2 tablespoons (110 g) unsweetened applesauce

⅓ cup (80 mL) vegetable oil

2 tablespoons apple cider vinegar

5 teaspoons red food coloring

1 teaspoon vanilla extract

Frosting:

½ cup (70 g) cashews

5 tablespoons (75 mL) unsweetened soy milk

1 tablespoon lemon juice

1 teaspoon apple cider vinegar

1 teaspoon vanilla extract

4 cups (480 g) powdered sugar (approx.)

2 tablespoons vegan butter

Pinch of salt

For the Cupcakes:

1. Preheat the oven to 375°F (190°C). Line a 12-cup muffin pan with paper cups or grease the cups generously with oil.

2. In a large bowl, whisk together the flours, sugar, cocoa, baking powder, baking soda, and salt. Set aside.

3. In another bowl, whisk together the soy milk, applesauce, oil, vinegar, food coloring, and vanilla.

4. Add the soy milk mixture to the flour mixture and stir to combine.

5. Using a ⅓-cup (80 mL) ice-cream scoop, divide the batter among the prepared muffin cups.

6. Bake for 20 minutes, or until a toothpick inserted in the center of a cupcake comes out clean. Remove the cupcakes from the pan, transfer to a wire rack, and let cool completely before frosting.

For the Frosting:

7. Soak the cashews in boiling water for 15 minutes. Drain.

8. Add the soaked cashews to a blender, along with the soy milk, lemon juice, vinegar, and vanilla, and blend until creamy.

9. Transfer the mixture to a bowl. Add the sugar, vegan butter, and salt, and whisk or use a hand mixer to beat to a smooth consistency. If the frosting is too thick, stir in a bit of water. If it's too thin, stir in a bit more powdered sugar.

10. Frost the cupcakes using a knife or a pastry bag fitted with a round or fluted tip.

ACKNOWLEDGMENTS

I first want to thank my wife, Amélie, without whom this project would never have seen the light of day. Her contributions to the creation of the recipes and the writing have truly made the book better. I could not live without this extraordinary woman, both as my collaborator and as my wife.

I would also like to thank the talented photographer Dominique Lafond for her creativity and professionalism; the excellent food stylist Michael Linnington for his artistic sense; and Mathilde Bessière for her support. I'm also grateful for the superb work by Studio Miles, artistic direction and graphic design; Caroline Simon, prop styling and accessories; Joëlle Landry, editing; Vincent Fortier, copy editing; and Virginie Baudrimont, editorial coordination. These acknowledgements would not be complete if I didn't highlight Jeannie Gravel's contribution as production manager. Thanks to Antoine Ross-Trempe for his trust and confidence. Thank you to Marie Asselin for her translation work, and Sue Sumeraj and Gillian Watts for copyediting and proofreading.

Thank you to Emma Parry and Ali Lake. Thanks also to Robert McCullough, Lindsay Paterson, Colin Rier, Michelle Arbus, Charlotte Nip, Talia Abramson, and the rest of the Appetite and Penguin Random House Canada team.

INDEX